Graywolf Press

THE
PERFECT
STRANGER

P. J. Kavanagh

Graywolf Press

Saint Paul,

Minnesota

1988

This is the first U.S. edition of The Perfect
Stranger. First published in Great Britain by
Chatto & Windus Ltd., and reprinted in paper-
back in Great Britain in 1973 and 1985.

Graywolf Press receives support for its publishing
program from a number of generous foundations,
government arts agencies, corporations and indi-
viduals, including the Minnesota State Arts Board
and the National Endowment for the Arts. Graywolf Press is a member agency of United Arts,
Saint Paul.

ISBN 1-55597-115-6
Library of Congress Catalog Card Number 88-81020
9 8 7 6 5 4 3 2
First Printing, 1988

Graywolf Press, Post Office Box 75006, Saint Paul,
Minnesota 55175. All rights reserved.

Or will one's wife also belong to that country

And can one never find the perfect stranger.

—LOUIS MACNEICE

Foreword

FROM TIME TO TIME, since this book was first published nearly twenty years ago, I have been asked to write a sequel, and I have always gone through the same two reactions to this request. The first is astonishment, that anyone having read the book should think such a thing possible; and the second reaction, which comes later, is that after all it is a reasonable suggestion, the book is a kind of narrative and everyone likes to know the end of a story.

But the story does end in this book, in a particularly final fashion; therefore any unsatisfied curiosity the reader might feel must be about me, about how my story continued. So why, therefore, the surprise?

The answer lies in the motive for writing this book in the first place and (pretentious phrase, but I hope to make its meaning clear) the relationship of a writer with his work. Although it may sound naive, it simply never occurred to me, putting these pages together so long ago, that I was writing a book that booksellers and librarians would feel impelled to put in the category 'Autobiography'. If the idea had struck me I should have stopped at once. What I was concerned with trying to express were two facts which had borne heavily upon me during the previous years; they seemed to contain a shape which demanded expression: the facts of love and death, great events we can all share. But they are not abstractions, they happen to people, and therefore to give them force and colour the people to whom they happen must be described. They are in a sense *impersonal* events (the impersonality I hope to explain in a moment) that impinge on personalities. But it is not the personality that is the significance.

I felt I had been shown something it was my duty to show, and share with, others. In order to do this I had to show myself, but myself was not the point (though I greatly enjoyed the showing). And, as I wrote, something else happened which suggested I was on the right track. I felt the events of the narrative—in many cases even the words—selecting themselves. The book (and this of course was a subjective experience and is not a claim, was dictating its own shape, was becoming a thing, quite apart from me and, though it could hardly be more personal, was acquiring yet another kind of impersonality. Therefore it has always been obvious to me that to add to it or change its shape in any way would be to tamper with a shape the material had demanded, and thereby reduce the whole attempt to the level of a reminiscence.

I hardly expect anyone to understand this. I barely understand it myself. Yet it is so. When someone who had just written and published a painful personal memoir said to me recently that he had written it with tears pouring down his face 'as you must have written *The Perfect Stranger*', I could only stare at him with astonishment, and was so startled I blurted out something like, 'No, on the contrary, I wrote it roaring with laughter', which is not entirely true, but is nearer the truth. So is it when people tell me how 'moving' they found the book. That is kind of them and I do see, because of the book's nature, why they would hesitate to say they found the book funny, but it would give me greater pleasure. For this is what I found, was surprised by, as I wrote: some kind of healing laughter below the surface, nearly out of earshot, but not quite.

However, I do say at the end, 'the rest of my life will be a memorial' to what happened (and the first title I gave the book was *A Memorial*), and the reader has a right to wonder what kind of memorial, if any, is still in process of construction. If I knew I would say. But when a poet-friend, finishing this book, hissed at me with the kind of aggression, even antagonism, that friendship can contain at important moments, 'Yes. *But what happened next?*', there was something in the force, the italicisation, of the question that I appreciated and understood. He meant 'What kind of insight? What source of extra knowledge?' did these events grant.

The truth is I have been sustained by these events, in a world transformed by them. Whether I have taken from them the full sustenance they contain or whether I have turned too often aside and failed in concentration, I do not know. But the sustenance remains, a miracle. That is why any account of my subsequent life which was not a wholehearted examination of this mystery would only be prattle.

A year or so after the time at which this book ends I became a professional actor, because I had some talent in that direction and precious little in any other, and I badly needed intense occupation and companionship. Some years after that I remarried and had two children and set up, as I had always wanted to, as 'a writer'. (My first act, that decision taken, or partly taken, was to write *The Perfect Stranger*.) So it has gone on, leading a family life in the country and now, with some hesitation, writing this. But it has all been a continuation of the glimpse, the gift I was given, however unworthy I am, and never a separation from it.

I have written about this in fragments, in poems and articles and broadcasts and novels, thinking of them as bricks, as piece-by-piece additions to the monument, not caring too much if anyone noticed, for the attempt is a duty, the success of the result is chance. Yet it has been a pleasure, as well as a frustration (for it is immensely difficult) to try to express some part of what I have termed the 'impersonality', but what is better termed the 'suprapersonality' that I feel at the heart of everything.

In other words, if I ever came to write a sequel to this book it would be theocentric, mystical, and that I do not yet feel prepared to do. Perhaps nowadays such matters are best expresed in glimpses, from different angles, in the hope that someone should come across some piece of it that has managed to get itself expressed and say with surprise, 'Why, that's what I feel!''

The memorial is still being built and whatever is wrong with it is what is wrong with me, is my fault. But the abiding value of the materials, which are not mine but come from without (and are in that sense 'impersonal'), is not in doubt, and every day I feel more assured. That assurance may be taken away, and the world become once more a blank. Even then the memory of what happened, and of the things that have arisen from it, would remain. Even if we should want to, there are certain things too strong for us to betray.

P. J. Kavanagh
1984

The Perfect Stranger

RECENTLY I HAD to make arrangements for my gravestone. This came about in a certain way, the result of things that had gone before, and I felt a need to write down some of those things before it was too late – after all anyone's gravestone is an understatement. And it seemed best to begin at the beginning I knew most about, in other words my own.

Certainly this is a personal book and perhaps that needs an explanation. Also it's a love story and surely we don't need another of those.

But because things happen in one way and not in another .this is sometimes their point; and so for fear of missing the point (buried somewhere under the facts and nowhere else) the facts as they happened it has to be, and not done up into fiction.

This has its advantages (saves you having to invent) but lands you in difficulty. There are those who have come too close for you to describe them in the way novelists use – you can't even see them, in any ordinary sense, although you see them better than anyone, but description gives a quite false idea of their distance. Even if you wanted to it's not in your power to cash in on their specialness.

What you can do, though, is describe their effect on you, and the kind of life it was that they stepped in to, and this is why there are so many I's and me's in the story. But maybe that's the most we can say about another person with any certainty; however we wish to celebrate them we only have the bits and pieces of ourselves to do it with.

.

I was thirty-three years old a few days ago and my blood on both sides of my family is Irish as far back as anybody can be bothered to trace. I was born and brought up in England, and not really among Irish people – I never knew my grandparents, and my four uncles were killed in the First World War – but this Irishness has always been important to me, I don't know why. People often claim a bit of the wild Celt on account of a Scottish great-aunt, or so forth, and when I was a boy I often said I was pure English just to show what I thought of this game – and I've never heard anyone else claim that, which is surprising. But I knew it wasn't true. I came of a conquered dissident race and I talked too much for it to be true. Certainly this feeling allowed me to fall in love with England when I was twenty-seven with a passion that wouldn't have been possible if I'd felt myself a native.

My father was born in New Zealand and brought me up to be more Irish than the Irish. And we did have some history of rebellion and uprising in the family, as well as six Cardinals I've been told, and of clinging to the True Faith. But the Irish, with blazing exceptions, I cannot like as a race; they seem to me a mean and envious lot.

My father, like most talented Irishmen, loved Ireland from a distance. His real passion was London. He knew it in loving detail and was only really himself when he was at large there. He used London as an Irishman uses Dublin; home was for recuperating in. He earned his living writing jokes – he was the scriptwriter for a radio show called ITMA, which was famous in its day, and so was he, and highly paid. At least he was when I knew him, but when I was born we were poor, genteel poor. Not that my father was genteel, he was the only truly classless man I have ever met in England, but he had been a medical student on an allowance; he gave up medicine, the allowance stopped, and he and my mother and my brother, and then later me, descended from houses to flats to digs to dingy boarding-houses; I remember one of those. My grandmother died early in this progress, and after her deathbed had been surrounded by clergy was found to have left her money to the Church, and her son and his wife and baby nothing at all. My mother has never forgotten this. During this moneyless period which continued for perhaps ten years, my brother (who is twelve years older than I am) remembers that my father just sat at home and read, his elbows and knees gradually becoming visible through his clothes. He never noticed things he didn't want to, and I suppose it was my mother who had to battle with the unpaid grocers and the landladies, and organise the moonlight flits.

He could be a very funny man, my father, and sing impromptu comic songs, and was in great demand for various unlucrative occasions. It took him twenty years to discover how to make a living out of what he did best, and that happened by chance.

In the very early days of radio he used to enjoy putting on his earphones and twiddling the cat's whisker on the crystal. One day he heard a comedian called Tommy Handley who made him laugh, so he wrote him a sketch and sent it in. (He remained all his life a connoisseur of comedians. When I was very young he used to drag me round the music-halls and down to the end of piers, and we would go back-stage afterwards where the comic always seemed to be sitting in his braces, morose, surrounded by Stout bottles.) It would be comforting to say that after this he never looked back, but it was a long time before he was at all successful, and after that his success waned a little; but it is a moment worth recording because a man had found his métier.

That is such an important moment it fascinates me. To some it never comes, and for others it is often pure chance. Tommy Handley himself began as a singer. Engaged to do a broadcast in the earliest days of 2LO at Savoy Hill, there was some microphone trouble during rehearsal and the engineers asked him to say something into it. He recited 'Thirty days hath September' and the engineers behind their glass panel began to laugh. The microphone did something unexpected to his voice.

In the interval of whisker-twiddling and reading, my father was a protégé of G. K. Chesterton and he earned an occasional cheque by writing for his paper, G.K.'s Weekly. He was also much concerned with a Catholic version of Communism which was in the air in those days. It was called Distributism and was probably a bit back-to-the-land-y and Tolstoyan. Like most fair-minded but impractical ideas, it slowly ground itself down, and the last Distributist I know croons nightly over a tiny compost heap in Haywards Heath.

•

I was born during the slump, when the family fortunes were at their most pinched. By the time I was old enough to care, it was wartime and everybody was pinched.

There was some rather splendid bombing in Bristol. We went down every night to the cellar-smell until one dawn a tin-hatted warden stuck his head through the grating and shrieked at us to 'evacuate.' Then we walked through the blazing city – even the barrage balloons were on fire in the sky – and I noted with satisfaction that my school was also burning. A young couple whom I liked used to read the Daily Worker in the cellar, and I remember my father pointing this out to my mother in a way that made me realise they were 'odd.' A sign, I suppose, that my father was moving to the Right with age, a remarkable and almost invariable phenomenon. Gladstone is the only notable exception I can think of, and then only on certain topics; Ireland for instance. Robert Frost once said that he was never a radical in his youth in case he became a Tory in his old age.

I also remember the house next door being on fire and hoses being played against the outside of our walls to stop them cracking, while my father sat writing. I don't know whether I admired him for this, or copied the admiration of my mother.

.

From the age of six until I was eight and the war broke out I went to school at a girls' convent in Barnes. I suppose the upbringing I had in England was like an Irish one in many ways, that is to say, Catholic. And the sense that gives you of being in a minority remains with you all your life. But if the people all round you don't share your special superstitions, neither do you share theirs. The nuns, for instance: they weren't sinister, mutilated figures but jolly, round-faced girls who hugged me and gave me things and seemed to be always laughing. Perhaps they were over-scrupulous, I don't really know. In a gentle little talk on stealing I remember a beloved nun of mine telling us that if we found even a pin we shouldn't keep it, but find out whose it was and give it back. For some time afterwards I went about with my eyes on the ground hoping for a pin I could give myself the pleasure of returning.

The big girls gave a performance of *Macbeth*, and in the Witches' scene I was fascinated and strangely moved by their bare pink feet padding around the cauldron. I kept creeping nearer to see these more clearly. I was about eight and constantly in love. I had a real passion for a huge, blouse-bursting Amazon called Bridget. I couldn't think how to express my devotion, so like an adult I decided really I hated her and threw an apple at her as hard as I could. It hit her in the eye. Rubbing one and looking through the other, she asked me to tea, which was just what I'd dreamed about snug in bed at home. It seemed, however clumsy one was, the beloved *understood*, in a way no one else ever could.

I was very spoiled. Girls my own age, and older, used to kiss me when I wasn't looking and then run away. This surprised and delighted me at the time and surprises me now because I was very far from beautiful. I once had a photograph of myself at this age in a much-prized navy-blue nap overcoat and cap to match. I looked like a little old man cut down, a wizened leprechaun. But what with the nuns and the girls and my mother I began to take for granted the love and forgiveness of women and return it with my whole heart. I needed women more than life itself; they were life itself, and when later I went to boarding-school and was cut off from them I wanted to die. I willed myself to. And then I took to hiding near the Matron's room (an elderly, cross moustache we called The Bitch) just to hear the rustle of her apron and the sound of her sensible heels, distinguishably feminine only to the loving, obsessed ear.

To my mother I owe a special debt of gratitude. For twelve years she tirelessly made me feel the centre of the Universe. When I felt the centre slipping at all I got her to walk behind me, as I strutted before in my beloved overcoat, and call out over and over again: Who is that *handsome* little boy? Who is that *interesting* little boy? until I felt better. At twelve she let me go my own way, with scarcely a struggle; this seems to me perfect; or, at least, uncomplicated.

All the spoiling I had was luck, a kind of preliminary bonus; it wasn't for being a good little boy. In fact I must have been horrible. I managed to knock out several of my mother's teeth with my head, on purpose, and tried the same trick on my brother, splitting his lip. The only thing I remember with pride is announcing that I didn't believe in God. This took courage because I'm sure I'd never heard of anybody who didn't, and it made me a minority of one. Of course I *did* believe in God, possessively, secretly. I suppose I didn't want my God confused with theirs.

At some stage during the bombing of Bristol I began to ponder the chances of Eternal Punishment and became very frightened indeed. My father was listening with his head cocked to the sound of the explosions which were only a few yards away. It seemed a good moment to confide my fears – that I hadn't been to Confession, wasn't in a State of Grace – which was all that mattered at such a moment I'd been told. Usually so gentle, he turned on me with a contorted face: 'Don't be so bloody silly!' he said.

I pondered his reaction and it rather cheered me up.

THE B.B.C. REMOVED to North Wales and we went with them. There I was very happy in a house that looked over the cheerful Menai Straits to the green-check bedspread of Anglesey. I went to a tiny libertarian preparatory school and was taught very well. The parachutist scare was on and I worried if I would be brave enough to defend my mother if a German soldier hammered on the door. Should we offer him a cup of tea, all hot and sweaty in his harness? I'd read somewhere that this was 'collaborating', but I felt I should be tempted to, unless he was a bully, and then I wasn't sure what I'd do. I dug a defensive trench just in case behind the coalshed. In the spring I sat out in the field at the bottom of the garden and played the Swanee whistle to the lambs to see if music could encourage them not to become as dull as their parents.

After school we played war-games in the steep woods that led down to the Straits, keeping in a group to protect ourselves from the Elementary schoolboys, who set on us if we ventured out alone. I was small but I had a reputation as a boxer, and the others used to enjoy setting me on to fight boys bigger than I was. I wished to be popular, above all things. One of our group, a big boy, became unpopular with the rest for some reason, and encouraged by the others I found myself fighting him. Even as we were poking at each other I wondered why I was doing it; I had no quarrel with him. Afterwards was the first time I felt sick inside myself, and frightened, as though I'd done something that had changed me and I'd never be the same again. I think it was the end of my childhood.

I stayed there three years and was happy except for that, and then I was sent away to boarding-school where I was very unhappy indeed.

.

No need to describe the commonplace brutalities of a third-rate English boarding-school. This one was Jansenist-Irish and English-Puritan all at once and seemed to isolate all the coldest elements of these until only the rules and the fear were left. Extraordinary, the sense of being watched. Once it becomes part of you it remains on your skin like a disease.

At the end of every corridor (we called them cloisters, it was a monastery school) there was always a black figure in long skirts and silent rubber shoes; at the end of the dormitory, at the back of the study-hall, at the end of the shrubberies near the cricket-field – the only place where we were allowed to walk – a stationary silhouette, glasses winking pruriently in the light, the expression at the corners of the mouth containing all the knowledge necessary of the fallen nature of man, and boy. The odd thing is that, watched, you feel guilty, however much contempt you summon.

'Come here!' Walking along the cloister a year later on the first day of term, trying not to cry in front of the others, I heard myself called from fifty yards away in the gloom. The figure remained perfectly still and expressionless until I was exactly in front of it, arms folded beneath the shiny, worn habit, entirely at ease, waiting. He looked down: 'Stop walking along the cloister as though you owned it.'

That moment still stuns me almost as much as it did then, a first hit in the face.

Not all the monks were as bad as that. The rest, for the most part, were good-humoured and incompetent. Any ninny who joined the monastery could teach as soon as he ceased to be a novice. Some of our classes were given by men who not only didn't want to teach but who'd sometimes failed to pass even the ordinary school examinations a couple of years before. For this our parents paid large fees. As the monks were of course not paid, and as the food was horrible, I can only presume the money went towards the building of the new Abbey Church in which we spent nearly the whole of our one free day attempting to praise God.

The school, being a Catholic one, was not subject to Ministry of Education inspection, otherwise I imagine none of this would have been allowed to continue. Nor would the food. It was war-time, and it must have been difficult, but there could have been no excuse for the terrible filth served up to us. Sometimes a whole refectory of one hundred and fifty hungry boys returned supper to the kitchen untouched and nobody, *in loco parentis*, seemed concerned that their charges went to bed hungry. It's so much easier complacently to concern yourself with someone else's soul.

But the monks suffered just as much. We'd see the younger ones shamefacedly stealing sour apples from the orchard, concealing them in their habits held up like aprons and running to the laboratories to cook them over Bunsen burners. I felt vaguely ill the whole time I was there and regarded it as a normal part of life. Compulsory Rugby after a succession of untouched meals is a misery without parallel in later life.

Cricket I loved, and the summer terms. The hairy-legged, hearty, slightly brutal monks who supervised Rugby would go into hibernation and a taller, more languorous breed would take their place, or so it seemed to me in my relief.

Cricket is often associated with a sort of self-conscious 'gentlemanliness' but to me it meant gentleness, a quality I thirsted after as I found myself becoming more and more violent.

We had an old Nottinghamshire professional called Shipston of unrelieved gloom. I never heard him give any coaching advice at all except: 'Joost stay there. Roons'll coom. Roons'll coom.' But even he couldn't succeed in making cricket dreary. Sometimes watching county matches or reading newspaper articles on the decline of cricket I remember Shippy and his invariable advice. The decline of cricket, if such there is, began a long way back.

.

My particular friend was Spud Murphy. He taught me to think I could distinguish between the songs of a garden-warbler, a white-throat and a willow-warbler, even when they were all singing together. He could dive into a thicket and uncover the perfect globe made by a gold-crested wren as though by divination. He made it seem so easy; I have often tried to do these things without him, but with no success. Thrushes' and blackbirds' and finches' nests were to him mere commonplaces; he'd uncover a dozen in the course of our too short walks. Once he discovered a meadow-pipit's nest – a real rarity that – in the middle of the Rugby field. And another time we had a feast of partridge eggs boiled over a fire we made ourselves. He made himself climbing-irons that he attached to the insides of his legs and clambered dizzily up into rookeries and came down with eggs in his mouth. He taught me how to hold a thin tube over a Bunsen burner, draw it out like elastic, carefully break it when it was cool and there you had two little pipes ideal for blowing birds' eggs. He kept a ferret and a Little Owl, in secret of course, and his favourite literature was *Exchange and Mart*, to which he used to send for all sorts of things to make hutches out of, and snares, and heaven knows what. He had a way with animals I've never seen in anybody else; he was like one himself. Together we won the Natural History prize two years running with our collection of birds' nests in their natural habitat. We waited till the chicks had flown and then we carefully extracted the still fresh nest, whole, cutting down most of the surrounding tree with it. It was one of the few things we should have been stopped doing. Spud swam the width of a gravel pit in his clothes and swam back drawing the huge stinking raft of a Great Crested Grebe's nest between his teeth. He was one of the most interesting people I have ever met.

Once when we were leaning against a luke-warm radiator on a particularly freezing day the Headmaster walked past. After telling us not to lean on the radiator and rebuking us for stuffing indoors, he looked at us both and said pensively and with no affection: 'Birds of a feather . . .' This was aimed at me and reflected on poor Spud, who took on even more of his furtive indoor appearance. I suppose in any school his virtues would not have been prized. He was nearly unteachable because he wasn't interested and soon left altogether.

My consorting with such a dullard and obviously rough fellow was a source of disappointment to the Headmaster, because he was an old friend of my father and expected better things of me. Quite what he never divulged. My father knew a great many rough fellows and would have particularly loved Spud. However, the disapproval and disappointment of this Olympian figure – at least he was a gentleman and a scholar and was strikingly handsome and had played cricket for Warwickshire – lay heavily on my snobbish and hero-worshipping schoolboy's heart. But by now it was all too late. I had turned inwards, I felt all the time, through a haze of resentment and fear and pig-headedness: 'All right if that's the way you want it,' and I kept all my vulnerabilities doggedly to myself.

I think I must have admired him because his ill-opinion was the only one that hurt at all. As we grew older we were allowed to sit in his study in the evening and smoke until the room began to sway and tilt with nausea. He sat at his desk examining *The Times* column by column, his pipe between his teeth, a picture of peace and the kind of continuity and connectedness that I longed for; surrounded by the drawings of Thomas Derrick, the Sargent sketch of Alice Meynell, and the framed doodles of his hero G. K. Chesterton, whom, I believe, he had received into the Church. It was in those days that he and my father had met. I longed to be approved by him, to talk to him, but I was not his kind of boy. And so I played up grimly to the picture he seemed to have of me and read my beloved Francis Thompson (his beloved too) wrapped in the lurid covers of a Bulldog Drummond novel: my defiances had become those of a slave. A year or so previously when I had been more successful than usual in my book-smuggling, when I had discovered Yeats and undergone the really tremendous excitement of *Prufrock*, he had written privately to my father that I continued to show no interest in intellectual matters. This filled me with a kind of despairing wildness. I didn't seem to be making contact with anybody. Between the self I walked about inside and other people there seemed to be a lens that played tricks – like the old-fashioned box-cameras you looked down into, at certain distances the image turned wrong way up.

.

There were monks whom I must celebrate: young Father Clement with his delicate Irish obliqueness; handsome Father Anthony striding along the cloister, his habit tied round him like a toga, covered in oil stains and sawdust from the workshop where we took crashed fighter-planes to pieces; Father Stephen who always looked as though he'd rather be having a siesta, but if he had to be awake then he was going to make sure we were awake too, and interested; puffing, nicotine-stained Father Dunstan who loved the theatre. And the two lay masters, Mr Greer and Mr Welch, who *knew* something and wanted to impart it and in their different ways actually liked boys. A litany of human beings, potent even against the penetrating dismissive glance of the migraine-ridden Headmaster.

Years later, when Father Ignatius was dying in hospital, my father diffidently suggested that I might visit him. But I wouldn't; to see me could have given him no pleasure save that of being remembered by an 'Old Boy'. And I didn't feel I was one in anything but name. I had forgotten these years, wiped them from my mind. And indeed until now when I have tried to give an impression of what they were like, I've scarcely thought of them. But they must have left their mark. For one thing, a paranoid attitude to authority – that no good was to be expected from it. And the slightly insane, or at any rate psychically dangerous concept of a private, un-shared bargain; you broke the rules, you were caught and beaten, and that was about the extent of your relationship with the grown-up world. I think I really preferred to be caught. Not that I wanted to be punished; I didn't feel I deserved it, but I had no desire to win: that would have implied a competition between us, a dialogue. I preferred total estrangement; always made a point of saying 'Thank you, Father,' after I was beaten (at one time I held the record for the number of strokes in a given period) partly out of bravado and partly to keep the terms of the bargain clear in my mind. Even my religion remained more or less intact, because authority's interpretation of it seemed to me ludi-crous and anyway a kind of trick. The virtue of humility, for example, was turned into a device to stop you asking questions of people who wouldn't have been able to answer them.

It was a cold world this created. I tried to keep warm by the faith, on slender evidence, that I had talent. If only I could hang on to what was inside me everything, eventually, would come clear.

WHAT HE GUESSED of this attitude made my father understandably impatient. I think he was afraid I was becoming some kind of snob. I probably was – a culture one. There wasn't a cultured atmosphere at home, there was certainly none at school, and I hungered for books and leisure and gentleness and was attracted to people who seemed accustomed to such things. Whereas my father had an observer's taste for life at its least pretentious. When I was eight he took me to Margate in a coach on August Bank Holiday. I remember deck-chairs soaked in beer and watching, unappalled, a very fat lady, very red in the face, climbing up one side of a donkey and disappearing down the other, over and over again. I remember the donkey particularly.

Now, possibly to counteract my snobbism, he sent me to Butlin's Holiday Camp to do a month as a Holiday Uncle, or Redcoat. I took my particular chum of the time, Captain of Cricket, Captain of Rugby, destined for a career in the Army. His marvellously easy acceptance of the world gave me comfort; I was cleverer than he was and so we protected each other.

·

I had to admit his red blazer and issue white flannels became him better. Mine didn't fit anywhere; the flannels, even with the turn-ups down, revealing a valley of grey dust, stopped somewhere well above my ankles, and the sleeves of my blazer rubbed uncomfortably against the knuckles of my thumbs. Thus equipped we retired to our chalet to prepare ourselves for the entertainment of the Campers. About our actual duties we were vague, but in the morning there was to be a sort of military briefing, so we would know then.

Ladies were sitting out in canvas chairs on the little covered verandah of the chalet-line. Soon we stopped our unpacking to sit on our beds and listen. They were the wives of the Squadronaires dance-band and were describing cosily, and in detail, what they did at night with their husbands, comparing performances. . . .

We hadn't guessed such things were, never mind that ladies talked about them. We listened till they had finished and then didn't care to look at each other, but with a muttered 'good night' turned to our first night's rest out in the big wide world; one of us, at least, not a little thoughtful.

·

In the morning, woken by the loudspeakers singing Commercials – 'Mars Bars are *Mar*vellous', etc, and do I imagine it or was there really one that went: 'Wake up! Geraldine and Gerald. Wake up! And read your *Daily Herald*!' – we went to meet our fellow-Redcoats.

These were bronzed PT Instructor-like men, or fat little round ones like failed pantomime comics; and hard-faced, good-looking girls in red blazers and white skirts before whose glance we felt miserably like the schoolboys we were. After a self-important pause the Camp Commandant strode in, left-right, left-right – aptly entitled with his newly-demobilised military glare. He began, sourly, to hum a little tune:

We're a little
on the rancid
a little on the rancid side.

Apparently not everyone was pulling his weight, no slackers allowed, etc. It seemed even adults had to sit through school-type pep-talks. In the end we were given our tasks and mine was to preside over a Coffee Dance in the Viennese Ballroom. It seemed pointless to confess I'd never been on a dance-floor in my life, and so, feeling and looking grotesque, I marched off in the direction indicated. Peter was put on Indoor Sports and there he stayed, happily winning the egg-and-spoon for the rest of our time there.

·

The Camp was divided into four Houses named after our Royal Dukes. At meal-times a leading Redcoat periodically jumped from his place and bawled something like: 'Who's going to win the Knobbly Knees competition?' and everyone had to shout 'Kent' at the top of their lungs. If it wasn't loud enough they had to do it again. Anyone who was chewing at the time and nervous he might choke had to pay a forfeit for not joining in; such as kissing the nearest old lady if he looked bashful, or running round the tables with his trousers rolled up to his knees if he looked vain. There was ample scope for sadism among the Redcoats. The chanting contin-ued: 'Who are a lot of sissies?' 'Windsor!' the roar would dutifully go up: 'Gloucester – Boo!' and so on. I wondered at the obedience of people who had presumably come here for a holiday; but many of them had little metal badges extending from their lapels to their braces-buttons, campaign medals of previous holidays at other, similar camps. 'Hi-de-hi!' came the scream from the bull-necked Redcoat at the top of the table. 'Ho-de-ho!' came the happy reply from several hundred throats.

From time to time blushing girls egged on by giggling friends asked for your autograph, which you scrawled with an absent-minded flourish. Who did they think we were? I soon learned to disguise my total ineptness on the dance-floor by smiling understandingly, a smile which implied a world of ballroom experience and knowledge of the latest dance-steps, hardly to be expected from anyone so young and obviously provincial as my partner. As far as I could tell this always worked. I never lacked for partners; indeed the girls fell over themselves to dance with a Redcoat, and if they got this one promptly fell over him. They used to stare, fascinated, at the patternless slitherings of my feet:

'Is that a kind of fox-trot?' they would ask humbly.

'Kind of,' I would answer, smiling into the middle-distance, humming knowledgeably to myself. At last, gratefully, we would sit the rest of it out. If my partner looked more than usually depressed I'd say hopefully: 'Like it here?' But invariably she would reply, with a dreamy roll of the eyes: 'Smashing!'

I was yet to find my soul-mate. I could find nothing to say to these girls, the first I'd mixed freely with, that didn't sound in my own ears like a parody of a bad film. I suppose they expected some kind of approach as part of the game, but even if it had occurred to me that girls were like that I wouldn't have known how to begin. Also my man-of-the-world act rather got in the way; one false move and I'd be out of my depth. Altogether the impression I made must have been very confusing.

The problem of how to make a beginning with a girl was much discussed between us in our chalet. It seemed insoluble because we took it for granted that nothing could be further from a girl's mind, you had to apologise for your baseness and at the same time convince her it was a good idea. We pondered this, getting nowhere.

The girl who gave the messages over the loudspeaker: 'Will Camper Brown please go to her chalet. Her baby is crying. Thank you', had a beautiful RADA sort of voice. (Snobbism again?) She lived behind a glass panel near the swimming-pool, and on secret inspection proved to be quite as pretty as she sounded. She must have hundreds of boyfriends . . . what could we do? After several days' discussion we marched in upon her at her microphone and invited her to tea at the Tudor Milke Barre. She was as amusing as she was pretty, and when we parted I was the proud possessor of my first girl-friend.

We were both thunderstruck she should so obviously have preferred me to the Captain of Cricket. I really believe I was as surprised as he was. But on her half-day there was Pauline in her huge New Look skirt, and soft, brightly coloured, scented blouse, more feminine than anybody ever was; and all the time she was making up her face, straightening her skirt, combing her long fair hair, she was doing all these things before coming out with *me*.

We were paid six pounds a week and spent it in Scarborough. Once, mingling the new pleasure with the old, I took her to Cricket Week. There, in the sun among the panama-hatted cognoscenti, Pauline went to sleep with her tiny cat-like head on my knees. Those around us looked cross, as well they might: they hadn't got Pauline.

·

Meanwhile the Butlin's duties continued; performed by me with increasing melancholy.

Every night at the end of Ballroom duty we Redcoats linked arms in a chorus line and, kicking our legs to the tune of 'Good night ladies', sang:

> Good night Campers, see you in the morning.
> Good night Campers, glad to see you yawning.

You must cheer up
Or you'll soon be dead.
For I've heard it said
That folks die in bed – So we'll say
Good night Campers, don't sleep in your braces.
Good night Campers, soak your teeth in Jeyes's.
Drown your sorrow (crescendo)
Bring the bottle back tomorrow.
Good night Campers – Goooodniiiight.

This last with our right hand upstretched, fluttering our fingers.

Most evenings I got through by talking to the drummer in the Squadronaires, whose gloom was so immense it made me feel almost hearty. (A conscientious drummer has an unrewarding life in a strict-tempo band.) I was glad to know his wife had not been among those overheard, and that I knew nothing he wouldn't like me to. Some of the others in the band I couldn't help examining more closely in the light of information received.

Every Saturday night there was a fancy-dress ball in which the Campers paraded in costumes new to them but very familiar to us. (There was a fresh lot of Campers every week.) It was always won, as far as I remember, by the man who clad himself entirely in enamel chamber-pots: The King of Po-land. Thus garbed he clanked round the edges of the floor all evening, alone; towards the end he usually looked as though he wished he'd come as a cowboy or an Apache dancer.

One night, on a sudden but pure impulse, I fled from the revelry of the Viennese Ballroom, rang my parents from a call-box near the roller-skating rink, and refused to go back for my last year at school. To my astonished joy there was scarcely a protest from the other end. It was over.

So was my time at Butlin's. I was called to the office of the steely Commandant.

'Why the hell are you here?' he yelled, almost before I was through the door.

'. . . Here?'

'Don't play bloody stupid with me! I know what you've been up to. Too many rough nights with that bit from drama school!'

(Not true, not true . . . we'd lain together on the sand in the dark with the other couples and she'd seemed so beautiful and delicate . . . even if I'd known how.)

'Why are you in this camp?'

'Er . . . to help people enjoy themselves?'

'*Exactly!*'

He threw a photograph across the desk. It had been taken by a wandering ballroom photographer and featured the King of Po-land. It also featured, well in the foreground, me; there was an expression of such cosmic sadness on my face that I saw his point.

However, he couldn't sack me from my first job because I was nearly due to leave anyway. But 'rough nights'?

WHEN I RETURNED home I found someone he'd met had sold my father the idea of a school in Switzerland, near Lausanne, and I was to go there. I was staggered. Treats were not common in my family, and my father was stern about other people's luxuries: 'travel light' he used to advise. My mother explained it was because I'd had a 'bad war', but whatever the reason I didn't stop to argue. I'd never see that awful place again. What was more, I wouldn't have to come home for the holidays, or at least not often.

Holidays at home completely defeated me, I could find no solution. We lived in a flat, too small for three, in Spanish Place, looking on to the huge blank wall of the Wallace Collection. I found it typical that our nearest neighbour should be a Museum. It's an area of frowning Victorian townhouses – Wimpole Street, Harley Street, consulting-rooms now for dentists and doctors; no one below the age of seventy seemed actually to live there. Even in its hey-day it must have been remarkably gloomy; Dickens devotes several pages of unfavourable epithets to it in *Little Dorrit*, and round the corner Mr Barrett behaved so strangely to his daughter. The place is a huge Bastille.

This was during and just after the war, roughly 1945–48,

and London was very dead anyway, but I'd never known it otherwise, and hated it. I had no friends at all, everyone I knew at school lived elsewhere; any money I was given went on cigarettes and endless, guilty, solo excursions to the cinema. I tried to read as much as I could, but the wireless or the television was always on and it was a very small flat. Sometimes I just walked up and down Oxford Street (surely one of the most horrible streets in the world?). I recited my terrible verses to myself as I wandered about; I even knew they were terrible, which didn't help:

> The ache in my heart
> is for life to start.
> Will it be long?

Even in its badness that contains some of the feeling of adolescent suffocation of those years; and self-contempt. I couldn't forgive myself for being so uncomfortable and so unhappy and not being able to find a way out. Looking back, I really don't think there was one, except to take a job, which is what I did as soon as I could. But I was heartily sick of my own company.

·

I can remember nothing of the journey – excitement must have driven it all away. Fragments of other journeys to and from Lausanne come into my mind: the couple who got into my compartment in the middle of the night somewhere in France, pulled a coat over themselves and promptly made love; the time I found myself going in the wrong direction, towards Prague I think, and had to clamber sleepily over the tracks, without French and without money, inhaling the smell of an undisputed 'adventure'. But of the first time, nothing; except fury, on arrival, to find that the only word I could understand was 'taxi'. I had no doubt everything else

I'd been taught was equally useless. Then I saw my new headmaster. I recognised him at once because he was like the little drawings in French school primers: 'Monsieur Gaston at table. Monsieur Gaston goes to the office', and Monsieur Gaston always wore a neat moustache and sharp knickerbockers just as this one did. We drove through the streets of Lausanne with their orange lighting which I'd never seen, out through pleasant tree-lined suburbs, and then we arrived at the school. I was shown to a large, shuttered room with two beds in it and an unfamiliar institution smell, told the time of breakfast and left to myself.

I sat on one of the beds (the other wasn't made up, the room seemed to be my own) and sniffed in the aroma of abroad. I was here, away, and as nearly as possible (time enough to find out about that) free. I went to unfasten the shutters which opened on to the two blank doors of a French window; these opened at last and I discovered a slatted wooden wall. I was disappointed but supposed new arrivals couldn't expect the best rooms. Then I noticed it was joined down the middle, pushed, and fell on to a balcony hanging like an open drawer over a lake the size of a small sea.

Just underneath were moored little boats clinking and gurgling in the moonlight, and the water between them sent up a soft, holiday smell of oil and ropes and varnished wood. The air was warm and powdery like it is after a hot clear day, although the water was surrounded by dark clouds continuing into similar coloured, lighter clouds until they frayed off into the clear central hole of the sky. I don't know how it was I became aware, slowly, that I was staring at mountains, with forests and animals and waterfalls, ending, I could see it now, in snow! There was a spare pair of lungs inside me that took a deep breath at that moment; it felt like their first. They were so full they seemed to press on my physical lungs until I couldn't breathe for joy. This was enough for me: a balcony, a lake with boats on it, and *mountains*.

•

I really don't know why that place existed at all. It was a sort of boy's 'finishing school' filled, at that time, with semi-refugees, Austrians, Hungarians, Czechs – there because they had lost their homes and their nationalities but not all their money, and Switzerland seemed a better place than most. In one or two cases the mothers, distinguished, fatigued-looking women, taught languages in the school to help out with the fees. But for them and their children it would have been understaffed and half empty. There were some Dutch, and several Swiss; studious pipe-smoking boys, the lights of whose rooms burned late into the night as they relentlessly studied for some Himalaya of a continental exam. There was one memorable Liberian, Alex Marazzani, whose lazy precision of speech I immediately made my model, and whose dark casual elegance I hopelessly tried to impose on my rufous, northern frame; all his slow gestures seemed to come from the centre and be completed, like a dancer's.

The rest of us were English and American; and by force of numbers, as well as by sheer volume of bad behaviour, we ruled the roost. The cliché of the gay, spontaneous Continental, and the sober, law-abiding Englishman was reversed; and no amount of sad lectures from the worried headmaster (who owned the school) about *'jeunes gens bien élevés'* and 'ambassadors abroad' made the slightest difference. Whether it was a rather nasty, unconscious pride of race or just a reaction against the particular strictness of our upbringing I don't know; but the Anglo-Saxons used that school as an hotel, and there was nothing this ambiguous Irishman could have liked better.

•

The lessons were as mysterious as the school itself. It took me several weeks (while my ears became attuned to the sound of French correctly pronounced) to discover we were being given a kind of business course, and that *comptabilité* meant double-entry book-keeping – I suppose they reckoned that toting up the profits was bound to become the major preoccupation of *jeunes gens bien élevés*. I arranged to skip the book-keeping classes and only go to the ones in French literature wherever these were being held. In practice this meant that no one knew where I was so I stayed in my room reading C. Day Lewis and Sartre, or even better, sat on my balcony, feet on the rail, looking at the mountains.

About eleven the maids came round cleaning the rooms and I learned my French from them. They were mostly Italian or Swiss-German and our careful, foreigner's French made it easier for us to understand each other. We worked out a marvellous scheme. Breakfast was huge jugs of chocolate, yellow-white unsalted butter, bowls of real jam (which I never remembered having tasted) and crisp, smoking rolls. Even this wasn't enough to get me out of bed in the morning (sometimes I read all night) but I regretted missing it. My room was opposite the back-stairs so every morning after breakfast was over one of the maids gathered up a few leftovers and smuggled them up under her apron. Breakfast in bed. . . .

I was learning French fast, my own way, and what was more I was enjoying myself. Joy pushed and jumped inside me as though at any moment I might give birth to a new and much better me. I decided to take Higher Certificate in case I wanted to get into a University; worked for it by myself, again in my own way, and don't remember doing any work at all, but I passed and so I must have. Where did anyone get the idea that pleasure was enervating, I wondered. What if it was? and anyway, it wasn't.

After a few weeks the spare bed in my room was filled by a walking prospectus of the international nature of the school, called Bob. His mother was Russian, his father Belgian, he'd been born in China and educated in the U.S. The predominant influence, as always, was the States; he had that clean-limbed, crew-cut, T-shirted look; he wore bright colours and blue Levi's and was altogether an object of admiration like an advertisement in *Esquire*; one of the two best-looking men I've ever known. The other looked very like him, Richard Selig the American poet, and with both of them, inevitably, I had fights. Quite affectionate ones, but fighting seemed the only way to adjust the balance of nature. I think the rivalry was animal, instinctive, not jealousy at all. Bob and I went everywhere together and when we met girls from the schools that are all over Lausanne I don't remember one of them ever addressing a remark to me. He transfixed them. They had photographs of him stuck up in their rooms (or so he told me). But also, I don't remember minding; it seemed only right and just, and I felt my turn might come.

Back in our room we played patience to see who was most in favour with Greenskirt or Headscarf, and his always came out and he'd chuckle with triumph. He infected me with his passion for this kind of fortune-telling and I've played it ever since; but it was only after I left the school I found he must have been cheating.

For the first time I wondered if I was meant to be a writer at all. The idea of being a 'poet' had taken root very early; no guarantee that it would become fact, but it was something to be clung to, a justification for the secrecy of my inner life – also I lived through poems. Until I was about twelve and had gone to boarding-school I'd found writing so much easier than anyone round me seemed to. It gave me a sense of power as though I was remembering something I'd always known; it's very difficult to forget that feeling if you've ever had it. This power (such as it was), this memory, seemed suddenly to disappear in adolescence, and the inside of my head became dull and sticky. But I'd been waiting for it to come back ever since.

Now, at seventeen, the age when Rimbaud was in full flight, I was full of glue. But if I wasn't meant to be a writer, what was I then? What would become of me? The question, really penetrating me for the first time, that I wasn't anybody very special after all, gave me a twinge of fear. I felt my moral courage was insufficient for the day-to-dayness, the mild waiting rhythm, contenting itself with half-pleasures and half-pains that made up most lives. I didn't think that such a life was beneath me; not really, I just thought I'd crack under it. I also knew my mind didn't function quite like other people's and that this worked both ways. There were areas in me of dark stupidity but sometimes I made connections and jumps that were different from theirs, which I couldn't explain. These were like bubbles welling up inside me, and if I couldn't get that excitement down on paper before it popped, what use was I?

.

But it was easy to put all such preoccupations to the back of my mind. We sat at cafés, and played uncompulsory soccer, and rowed at daybreak on the pink and green cellophane of the lake. In the evenings we drank cold beer flavoured with brandy in sweet-smelling light-brown pubs which all seemed to possess a pretty daughter. I was afflicted by my usual shortage of cash and did the only thing possible; got into debt. I still have the green corduroy jacket (daring, Continental garb) to this day as far as I know unpaid for. But I felt so fine and tall in it, so *artistic*, that after only five bus-journeys into Lausanne during each of which an exquisite Indian girl stepped demurely on and stood with downcast eyes next to me I plucked up courage during the sixth and spoke to her. Amazed at my daring I asked her to the best coffee-shop in Lausanne and there I bought her the biggest and creamiest invention of the Swiss genius. I was a little depressed by her relentless Anglo-Oriental good manners and the way she ate the cake as though she was used to such things; but she was very beautiful. When the bill came I found I hadn't enough money. . . . Politely she paid the difference and we walked back to the bus-stop, in silence. I put her on the bus, having just enough presence of mind to make another date with her by the statue in the main square. She turned away as soon as the bus began to move. It had seemed impossible to borrow my bus-fare from her, so as soon as it was out of sight I followed on foot. Next week I was at the statue, pockets bulging, a pair of trousers sold, and a book. I waited for three hours but she never came.

·

As soon as it was winter we went up into the mountains; the same ones I stared at every day. The school took over a small hotel in a tiny, untouristy village and there we did our lessons as usual, and learned to ski.

The smell of pines, and wood-smoke; the taste of the air, sharp and sweet, like a lemon water-ice; the mountains, coloured cut-outs in the morning, gaining volume and presence as the sun rose higher and turning Technicolor pink at night long after the rest of the valley was dark; the log fire in the hall of the hotel that gave out another kind of warmth to the one you already had on your cheeks; the tiny rooms with double windows and a huge, fluffed-up feather bed you disappeared inside when you lay on it, pulling over yourself an equally huge feather bolster until you were in a vast white sandwich of air and feathers; the pendulum weight of ski-boots, worn all day. There were girls there too, sisters and cousins staying for Christmas, mostly American and often divorced and to my eyes of unexampled chic, with fascinating international voices. We drank our brandy-flavoured beer among mahogany-coloured locals who broke their silence seldom through the facial hair and the cheroot. They watched impassively while we danced to 'La mer' or 'Douce France', Charles Trenet on the wind-up gramophone, or jerky, jumpy local accordion tunes that were easier to dance to in ski-boots, clump clump. Then out into the clearness of the night, cut off round us by the defined black points of the mountains; the crisp ice under our skis as we walked, slid, home; falling often at first and laughing.

We were there for three marvellous months and then the snow began to melt and we followed it down, back to the lake. I never really learned to ski. I couldn't find the courage to alter my balance in the way that makes you turn properly; it always felt as if my ankles would break. I discovered it took less courage to go straight and fast so I put my skis together at the top of the run and tried to stay upright until I reached the bottom. This gave me an undeserved reputation for recklessness which I enjoyed very much. As I went down fast – faster even than the instructor dared – I knew I wouldn't hurt myself because I was too happy.

IN LAUSANNE (Port de Pully to be exact, a village on the outskirts) all went on as before except it was summer. Bob played Claude Luter on his gramophone loudly now, with the balcony windows open, to attract the attention of any passing belles taking a lake-side stroll.

I had an advantage over Bob, and the others: every Sunday I went to Mass, and there I met a plump little Swiss girl. If I arrived late there was usually an empty place beside her, and if I was first she nearly always sat beside me and I was very conscious of the pressure of her side against my side, the scent of her white Sunday gloves, the rustle of her crisp Sunday blouse. After Mass we walked back along the sunny suburban roads, me talking in my halting French and loving the bright colours she wore and the sense she gave of airing cupboards and newly-baked bread; the lakeside finishing-school girls, for all their talk of Mummy and Daddy, their social pretentiousness, sitting on their dull virginity like a golden egg, gave the impression of being held together by grubby pieces of perished elastic. We walked as far as her father's shop and there we parted. I never knew her name, but her simplicity and unaffectedness were just enough for my fantasy to feed on, and anyway there was always next Sunday.

It began to get hot, the term came to an end, people left, or went on holiday. I stayed on to take my exam and after that there seemed less point in my idle life, no reason to do the whole sequence over again; this particular lemon had been sucked dry. My call-up for National Service had arrived, but that felt very far away, and as long as I was abroad I was deferred. Anyway the last thing I wanted was to go back to England – I was beginning to feel alive. But I'd learned (largely through Bob) that Switzerland was not the real thing; the nearest example of that was Paris, so there I decided to go. I began negotiations with my father for the money to get me there. He surprised me by agreeing – even approving; then he did more – he found me a job with a steel firm that had a branch in Paris. It was vaguely thought I might be able to translate letters; but anyhow, so it was arranged, and quite as excited as I was he decided to come over and see me settled.

·

I had never been that long alone with my father before; he shied away from intimacy with anyone, I think, and my attempts at it embarrassed him. I suspect I embarrassed him permanently, as though he never knew whether to agree with me (we were obviously so similar) or to disapprove, for the same reason.

He turned out to be the marvellous companion I'd always thought he might be. Not instructive and guide-like, as I imagined most fathers were, but delighted and fascinated by everything just as I was. (Although it was here he gave me the only piece of general advice he ever ventured, gravely pointing out the wisdom of a bottle of Vichy water by the bedside.)

He had a passion for coach-trips and conducted tours; he

was the least 'superior' man I've ever known, and he not only enjoyed the trips (which was the easiest way to dispose of the sights) but enjoyed the other people on them, and allowed them to enjoy him. So it was we wondered together at the stained glass in Sainte Chapelle, were horrified by Robespierre's study (was it?) and had a pot of tea afterwards with a pleasant couple whose greatest pleasure in Paris was to have found a foot-bath by their bed; in Montmartre we spent an evening with a car-salesman from Nottingham who besought us to visit the Sacré Coeur because it was new – Notre Dame, he assured us, was on the way out. (With my father it was always a case of Nature imitating Art.) We even went to the *Bal Tabarin* together on a 'Paris by Night' trip, and I saw my first naked girls; but I didn't stare as much as I wanted to for fear of embarrassing my father, and he seemed rather disequilibriated himself.

It was arranged I should stay temporarily in the flat of one of the chiefs at my job, whose wife was away; and so, his responsibility over, I went with my father to the airport. There he astonished me by giving me fifty pounds (for emergencies) and by appearing sad and subdued to be leaving me. And as he limped away on his newly-mended ankle, broken on an icy pavement after a winter's night session, his large black hat at its usual slight angle, I astonished myself by feeling sorry to see him go, as though he were a friend I'd not quite made – someone who could help me but who stayed out of reach – and that maybe the fault was partly mine.

·

The flat was huge and dark and incomprehensible. I couldn't find the light switches and there was a bicycle in the bath. The owner, always out or away, clearly didn't want me there and I promptly got a bad dose of 'flu. I lay in the dark and waited for it to pass. In the end I found the light switches but it made no difference because in those days there were almost continual power-cuts. About once a day I shuddered across to the bar opposite to dip a croissant in coffee and find out what time it was. It occurred to me, 'flu-depressed, that not for several hundred miles was there a soul who cared whether I lived or died. I'd broken the thread at last.

My host came back and barked at me. He always wore a charred yellow Gauloise stuck to his bottom lip and was very difficult to understand. He obviously wondered what he'd been landed with and I recognised this was no way to start my first job (not counting Butlin's). So I pulled myself out one morning at half-past seven, and five days and twenty minutes late, reported for work.

.

Naturally they didn't know what to do with me. I'd been foisted on them from above and they suggested delicately (they were quite kind) that the problem was mine, not theirs. To them I was some rich man's son: the whole matter decided over brandy and cigars – 'Send the young shaver to us, old man, send him to us'. I wondered how my father had in fact managed it; he remained all his life innocent and ignorant of wire-pulling and influence, although capable of taking literally a vaguely intended offer. Anyway there I was in an office attached to a factory in the only ugly part of Paris (near the Métro station Convention, and I liked the ugliness) quite incapable of being any use at all. I was at first given letters and technical brochures to translate from English into French, but only an engineer could have known what they meant. After preliminary exasperation and despair, trying to make myself as useful as I could, I was reduced to dusting the filing-cabinets. The rest of the time I spent talking to the pretty secretary whose room I shared. She gave me lessons in Parisian *argot*, but what she taught me, I discovered later, was very genteel.

I'd been led to believe that the British worked and foreigners talked, waving their arms about as often as not. This, like so much else, turned out to be untrue. We began at eight-thirty in the morning and finished at six, Saturdays included. Everyone arrived on time and no one left before time, and this made a long day for the filing-cabinet duster. He broke it up by popping out as often as he dared, a few minutes at a time, to look at the streets, to take a swift beer standing at a zinc bar, sniffing out the distinctive flavour of working Paris. The secretary explained his absence by saying he'd gone out *'pour jeter un coup derrière la cravate'* – and soon I gained a reputation as an alcoholic freak. When it was remembered that I was Irish – No, not *Holl*andais, *Irl*andais – all was explained. I became not the first of my (almost) countrymen to cash in.

Most of the people I came across in the office and the factory – the bosses – were, I discovered, Communist. What I saw made me admire them very much; the way they refused to take injustice for granted and the sinewy, practically-orientated hope they seemed to exude. This went some way towards explaining the huge bivouac-like flat, unlived-in. For its owner it was a transit camp; life was here in the office and on the factory floor, comfort could come later. I admired the sense this gave of being in the front-line, preoccupied wholly with the present. In his baggy suit, his nails bitten and yellow with nicotine, my host barked orders as one having authority. There seemed no distance between him and his men, and yet he was very hard on them, he didn't leave the driving to an underling. The way they spoke to him, arguing, sometimes throwing down their tools, only emphasised the impression of partnership. There was no division between the office and the factory, everybody was equally concerned with getting a particular order completed and they knew at the workbench what it was they were making, who for and when by; so far as I could see nobody performed a repetitive task that was meaningless to him. We all ate together at trestle tables put up on the factory floor – a good lunch, very cheap, with delicious coarse red wine; workmen in greasy overalls sat next to white-bloused typists and besuited office workers with what seemed to me perfect naturalness. Or rather I realised how unnatural a similar juxtaposition would seem in England, and that this awkwardness, however politely concealed, was not necessary, not a part of life.

Considering what he must have thought of me and of my being there, my host was kind. We occasionally walked back together after work and he asked me questions about England I wasn't able to answer. Once he sighed and said he wished he worked in London; there people took their time, sat in little pubs and talked, letting the world go by – whereas in Paris. . . . He constantly stopped to buy newspapers, tearing them open, his head held back to stop the eternal cigarette-smoke from getting in his eyes, snorting, grunting, muttering curses. Politics were his life and this made him enviable to me, a little heroic.

I moved into a very cheap hotel indeed. I couldn't hang around that office for ever, and that fifty pounds might have to last a long time. Bugs came out of the wall-paper, but I didn't spend much time with them. All day I was at the office, and in the evening until late I walked about.

The evenings fell into a pattern. First, a meal: I was discovering the joys of eating, not very adventurously – pork chop, which I'd never tasted (meat was still rationed in England) seemed difficult to improve on, so I had that every night. Then I went to some part of Paris I didn't know and walked around a bit, taking glasses of wine standing up in bars. I was too shy to go into the ones where everybody seemed to know each other, or those that had small entrances so you couldn't see what they were like inside, so I was left with the brightly-lit anonymous ones where men threw their drink down in one gulp and hurried away. I watched the deft barmen flicking and rinsing the thick-stemmed glasses, clanking them on their little saucers with a precise flourish, and pouring from the bottle, without looking, exactly to the brim. I liked the way they showed off, and thought of England where you weren't allowed that extra gesture of relish, that was often so beautiful.

In the morning the secretary always remarked on my appearance (normal for me at 8.30 in the morning) and suggested knowingly that I'd been out on the tiles with yet another *petite amie*. (I was beginning to guess her *argot* was not the one I wanted.) I assured her that this wasn't so, would even have offered her the job if she hadn't been married, but whatever I said she, and the others, knew better. I'd become a sort of mascot. I think they all considered me a little cracked.

I talked to people sometimes, joined them at their tables and so on, but I felt I wasn't creating a world for myself, or entering anyone else's. Once an English woman picked me up at the Café de la Paix and then kept examining me out of the corner of her eye. I could see her pretending to look ahead and then swivelling her pupil to the side. Whether she was nervous about me making a pass at her, or was nervously contemplating a pass at me I don't know; her self-consciousness so exacerbated my own that I slipped away.

Of course I knew you could pay for companionship, but although in those days I tried all the time to live and feel like a Hemingway character, the idea of making a transaction like that depressed me. I believed some men even preferred to pay, it made them feel superior and detached. I couldn't see this – surely if you had to pay a girl it put her in the superior position – I always felt abashed in front of lavatory attendants for instance – and I'd be worried whether I'd given her too little or too much, or whether I had enough – of everything. What with worrying about my pocket and whether I was going about things properly I didn't see how it would be possible to enjoy much, and anyway I believed girls who sold themselves seldom did so for pleasure (if they did I wouldn't have minded helping out) so I'd be trading on somebody else's forced choice in a corrupt economy. It didn't seem at all inviting.

But who knew? Just by walking around, not forcing anything, I might come across the right face, the right smile, frank exchanges reflected in the mirror behind the bar, no words spoken, perfect mutual understanding. That was the thing. But sometimes I did catch an eye in the bar mirror, and there'd be a smile that seemed to me false and cold, and although I'd ask myself why it should be anything else – this is a corrupt economy – if the head in the mirror jerked invitingly towards outside I'd hurriedly finish my drink, smile with deliberate gentleness directly at her, hoping she'd take me for queer and not feel rejected, and move to a different bar where I'd kick myself for another opportunity missed. Not for anything would I be eighteen again.

Sometimes I wondered, without much conviction, if all this wasn't a mere middle-class scruple, and made vows of amendment. Tomorrow I'd wake up a cool-eyed observer of the by-ways of the human spirit, in the dirtiest stews I would have my place, in the coldest debaucheries. . . . Wandering around Montmartre late one night, rather drunk, trying to feel as recklessly dissipated as I imagined Baudelaire must have felt, or Rimbaud, or even poor Francis Thompson, I was startled by an old woman hissing at me from a doorway, jabbing her finger upstairs excitedly. I wondered if her house was on fire; then I realised it was a brothel and hurried past, quickening my steps, as though the Hound of Heaven himself was after me.

I decided it would be a change for the better if I found a more cheerful place to live. Somehow I got myself a large, bright room, with a balcony, on the Avenue de Villiers. This was a more respectable neighbourhood than suited my fantasies, but you could just see the Sacré Coeur if you stuck your head a good way out of the window, and it was cheap. Very cheap, because part of the rent was to be paid in English conversations with my landlord. Our negotiations were very confused as he insisted on talking English, to the admiration of his wife, and he didn't know any. Much stress was laid on the *polishing* nature of the conversations we would be having, and the price was fixed accordingly. As soon as I moved in the subject was tacitly dropped between us, unless his wife was in ear-shot, and then I had to pretend I understood what he said.

One night I fell into conversation with a young English couple, a journalist and his wife, on holiday. They were attractive people and curious about my story; I must have played down the less successful bits and played up the rest because they recruited me to show them, as a resident, the 'inside' of Paris. The outside of Paris had been more than a match for me; I hardly knew the name of a street, I just wandered about aimlessly, enjoying myself sometimes, other times not. That kind of thing is difficult to admit, or make other people believe. I rummaged furiously in my mind for the stories Bob had told me about the Left Bank, Saint Germain des Prés, the *Caves*. Our beloved Claude Luter, bait for the lake-side girls, had played in one that Bob said was the best . . . the *Vieux Colombier*, that was it. Wondering how I was going to find it and whether you had to be a member, I volunteered to take them there.

We got in all right and although (as always) I'm sure the best, the original post-war days were over – this was 1949 – and although we were nearly forced to buy whisky, brand unidentifiable in the gloom, even to my romantically suspicious eye it was very nearly the real thing. Along the walls sat young people drinking water or Coke. The girls, barely discernible through the smoke and dark, were pale and serious – they had a white-faced, dark-eyed look that came to London about thirteen years later; and the men were the same age as they were – gaunt, fringed, relaxed. This in itself was marvellous to see. Whenever above ground I'd seen a beautiful girl she's been accompanied by a little fat man with stubby fingers. Dream girls, I was beginning to suspect, were as much a commodity as anything else. But here the young were together and formidably at home. They felt free to wander about, in and out, talk or not talk, even, in one instance at least, to sleep. None of them felt the need noticeably to respond – this was a place to shed strain, not take it on. To me it was miraculous to see so many people being themselves in a public place and surrounded by each other. England was a dreadful place to be young in.

Two or three couples boogie-woogied in the tiny space in front of the band. Thin, exquisite Negroes and rapt silent girls – dancing with abandoned precision, machine-like yet fluid; beautiful to watch, impossible to imitate. And to what music! A foot away from the dancers, two or three inches above them, smiling happily nowhere in particular, the greatest of all post-war jazz musicians: Charlie Parker, The Bird.

Sometimes he played by himself, to himself. He made stops, starts, grunts, hesitations in mid-phrase, turning the expected on its edge; he wandered off into territory of his own, came back, went off again in another direction, never losing the thread, relating all his journeys, in a way that was never obvious but always worked, to the original idea. For me his music was unlike any other I knew at the time because it took jumps, confronted similarities and contradictions exactly and unsentimentally, but was never cold. I'd heard him before and he always filled me with a kind of despair, because he played the way I would have liked to write, and this wasn't possible for me or anyone else. He made poetry seem word-bound.

After a while my friends had had enough and went back to their hotel, with many promises of something they were going to do for me tomorrow. I stayed on to listen some more and because I had an idea. It was now or never if I was to make contact with the world I felt I belonged to; enough of this wandering around alone. I did the sort of thing I've never been able to do since. I walked over and made myself known to The Bird.

He greeted me as a long-lost friend. . . . Taken aback, I searched my memory to see if we'd met . . . there'd been that concert in Lausanne, but there were a thousand other people there . . . I didn't quite catch what he was saying but apparently he was finished and I invited him for a drink, hoping he didn't drink whisky. He agreed happily and we went out together into the morning.

We never really got to the point of having a drink; we never really got to the point of anything. He talked all the time as we walked along, but somehow I couldn't pin down what he was talking about. I wondered at first if it was his Negro-American accent, and then I'd catch a sequence of ideas, make a reply, he'd agree enthusiastically, enormously good-natured, and then I'd find we hadn't been talking about that at all. And yet the words he used, that I didn't understand, and the way he used them, excited me. They suggested a world full of connections, that my limited meanings and old tired words cut me off from. I considered for a moment if he was drunk, but he wasn't like any drunk I'd met. He talked like he played, but with the connecting thread left out. I can't remember how we parted except that we might have known each other all our lives, or never have met, and for a moment both seemed the same.

'See ya tomorrow, man,' his cry came floating back down the empty street in the dawn, his eyes looking nowhere, not talking to me or to anyone, very happy.

He was high I suppose, and the words I couldn't understand were the beginning of Hip. He died not long afterwards.

It was true I'd spent the small hours with The Bird. I hadn't funked the original impulse this time. But back in my room I thought about it and I decided it wasn't as easy as that. You had to follow the clues inside yourself, even if they led to incoherence, to craziness, and people happened to you on the way. You didn't collect them, like stamps.

•

Next day I was taken by my new friends to meet Sturge Moore. I suppose he had a first name but I always knew him as 'Sturge'. He was about fifty, large, untidy, abstracted, with a magnificent head and horrible teeth. Whenever he climbed into a jacket or an overcoat he contrived to get the collar inside-out and stuck somewhere towards the small of his back. He continued to wave his imprisoned arms about, like stumps, without breaking the flow of his talk, until some adoring woman put him to rights. He was formidably intelligent, son of Sturge Moore the 'nineties poet, and he ran the English section of Radiodiffusion Française. I liked him very much and he treated me with courteous suspicion. We went round the corner of the Champs Elysées to an ugly little bar full of pin-tables and tarts which served him as an

extra office. There he held court among the expatriate painters and writers and bums who did odd jobs for the radio
under his patronage. What struck me about them was their
unphoniness, at least in front of Sturge; he had a quick eye.
I felt I'd stumbled across an unselfconscious bohemia
founded on the desire to work unhampered, or perhaps not
to work at all; what I was looking for in fact.

Sturge asked me to read the News, which I did. God knows
if anybody ever listened to us. We had 'request' letters, even
congratulatory ones; but I always felt they were written by
Sturge's girl-friends, or even Sturge himself, though I was
never sure of this. Soon I was reading it regularly and writing
pieces of scripts. (Sturge always cut out my jokes and I
decided he had no sense of humour. I remember some of
those jokes and he was very kind to keep me round the
place.) I also acted small parts. I gave up my job at the steel
works and felt that at last I was making my début into real
life.

The hours suited me perfectly. I went along to the studio
fairly late in the evening, finished around eleven and then
sat in the bar drinking Pernod and listening to the others
talk until late. After that I'd go home and read and sleep
and then wander out, blinking like a nocturnal animal,
pleased to be looking for my breakfast while everyone else
was having his lunch.

I lived in a silly, delicious dream; chanting Péguy, and
Claudel, building a religion for myself, sorting out what
didn't help. I'd tried not to believe in God – no one I re-
spected did, and this seemed to help them to live with themselves and with others as they were, not as they should have
been according to some deadening spiritual arithmetic – I'd
tried, hard, but I couldn't honestly claim to have succeeded.
I suspected not many people could honestly claim it – whatever they believed they didn't believe they'd usually filled

the gap with another irrationalism that seemed to me less rewarding. But still I wanted to be one of them, and dreaded the approval of the others whom I didn't respect. It would have been so much easier to chuck the whole lot away, there was so much rubbish among it; but I couldn't honestly do that, to my rage.

I wove a cocoon of prayers as I walked about – mostly for myself. I made a cult of Sainte Geneviève, patroness of Paris, about whom I knew nothing at all but felt that her job, looking after the problems of a crowded, fleshly city, would have given her the experience to help me with mine. I asked her to make me a poet, and to give me the courage to stay one; just as at school, a stunted, spotty fourteen-year-old, I'd prayed to Saint Jude, patron of Hopeless Cases, to make me tall and attractive to women.

Sometimes, after delivering my request to Sainte Geneviève in the barbarous, prehistoric cavern of the Sacré Coeur – maybe the car-salesman had been right and Notre Dame was on the way out, there was certainly something pagan about the Sacré Coeur – I stood on the terrace outside, at dusk, looking down over the lights of Paris, and felt tears building up inside me. I was alone and didn't believe I'd ever be otherwise. My life seemed a series of subterfuges to keep my 'inner life' intact, which made me mysterious to other people without being especially interesting. I'd somehow built a barrier round me it would take an exceptionally determined person to break through, someone who had a genius for love, and why should such a person single out me? Yet I believed I was simple, and probably I was. This emotion I felt – the vague, over-wrought longing of youth – I knew it was that and didn't rate it very high. I was aware of the sentimentality. But I was also aware of a kind of softness it would be easy to lose – that it might take great hardness to preserve. Even if the tears and the prayers separated me from the hard, fighting men I admired, and seemed to ally me with the lazy-minded grovellers I despised, if the tears and the prayers wanted to come I'd try to be strong enough to let them.

.

Now that I had so much time during the day I enrolled myself at drama-school behind the Hôtel des Invalides. Towards the end of my time at school I'd found I was quite a good actor. As Drinkwater in 'Captain Brassbound's Conversion' I'd made the Headmaster fall out of his chair laughing – but then he laughed as much when he saw me batting – and I'd found the laughter, coming up at me from the dark, guiltily exciting. Guilty, because I couldn't reconcile it with my ambition to be a poet. The part of me that exulted in performing seemed to make the part that was a poet shrivel up in priggish disgust and become very difficult to find again. I saw it as a tiny sprouting shrub hidden somewhere at the centre, extremely critical of the other parts of me it had for companions. None of these must be allowed to develop too far or they might stifle it altogether. One had to be constantly on the watch, I wasn't quite sure what against. Self-indulgence was an enemy, so were over-precision and dry mathematical exactness I thought. These stopped the mind floating when it might have floated somewhere unguessed at. I even tried not to learn the name of streets or useful buses, tried to keep everything in what I hoped was a fertile haze – reduced my brain to a sort of scrambled egg.

Nevertheless the theatre attracted me, in spite of the backstage glimpses my father had been careful to give. He snorted dismissively if I so much as mentioned my interest. (He had himself run away from home to join a travelling troupe until he was pursued and brought back, but I didn't know this at the time.) This school was talked about as the most advanced, so I went along. There was a delay of two or three months before I could take an audition, but I was welcome to come twice a week to the general class.

It was run by a retired *Comédie Française* actor called René Simon. What he was like at close quarters I never got to find out, but on these afternoons he gave an extraordinary and thrilling performance.

The tiny auditorium quickly filled with students dauntingly Student-like; gay, carefree, obviously devoted to the Highest in Art and dressed accordingly, they made me feel like the man who'd come about the smell on the landing. The boys had an ease with the girls which I carefully studied and the girls made me gasp. I never had courage or occasion to speak to any of them.

After we were all assembled and not another body could be crammed in, an expectant stillness settled and Simon strode on to the stage as if he'd just hurried from a train. He was a grey-haired, handsome man of about fifty with an actor's strongly marked but anonymous face, neatly-dressed, not tall, and gave the impression that he cared far more for what he was saying than he did for himself. As what he was trying to communicate is nearly incommunicable, not facts so much as a state of grace, this histrionic selflessness had a huge impact. I suppose he played God to us, but he did it very well.

He began quietly, talking of some class that had taken place earlier, addressing his students by Christian name, calling into the darkened auditorium for them to make themselves seen. These he'd chide or praise, but not for work done or undone, not even for quality (he was the first adult I met who despised competition) but always for the same thing – the extent to which they'd dared to expose whatever was vulnerable in themselves. It's obvious that this is the really difficult thing, and no good work can be done without it, but it is usually muddled up in sermons to the young with morality and duty and 'religion' formulated in such a way that they constitute an escape, not an astringence. We listened attentively while he tried to teach us to strip the layers from the only bits of ourselves that might contain the slightest interest. Sometimes he called one of the students on stage and once he thrust his fingers into the short curls of a girl and savagely twisted her face round to the audience demanding that we look at her. He commented on her appearance and anatomy and did a brutally exact imitation of how she was standing, of the impression she gave of being withdrawn, self-hoarding. Then, pulling her upright, shouting at her to open her eyes and look out, he startled her into anger and we all suddenly saw what was there, the beauty, and what she had been keeping from us. I'd flinched at first from the cruelty, but its truth was so obvious, and so relevant to us all, that nobody could mind, not even the girl, whom now he was dismissing with a kiss and calling his *petite constipée*. From there he went on, mainly about life in general, with growing passion, shedding his jacket and tie, unbuttoning his shirt, as he went along. He'd reach his peroration, usually a piece of Corneille, covered in sweat, his hair standing on end, grab his jacket and rush off as suddenly as he'd appeared. He really wasn't there to sell himself, but the best that had been done in the past and always in terms of the present; the only spellbinder I've ever come across who was on the right side.

As I'd rejected pretty well every teacher I'd been given and hadn't enjoyed doing that, I tried to define what was different about this man. He was specific; he didn't preach, he gave you tips. For example, if you must smoke use French cigarettes, not English or American, these contain too much saltpetre; girls, don't sit too long on the bidet, give nature a chance, overcleanliness is a form of fear. The young have an insatiable appetite for this sort of thing and hardly ever get it; concrete advice, nothing to make you a better citizen, only to make you more alive. Sometimes a student came to him and said (here he imitated a self-pitying whine that made me wince, I'd heard it in my own head): 'I don't *know* anybody! How can I get to *meet* people?' Why didn't he go into the nearest bar and talk to the first person he liked the look of? Always seek out the company of those you can learn from, and so on.

My one personal encounter with Simon makes me wonder if I was naturally as unteachable and bloody-minded as my schoolboy days made me suppose. I was waiting in the foyer among a crowd of students all of whom knew each other and I'd stuck a cigarette jauntily in the corner of my mouth to show I didn't mind being out of things. Passing, he flicked it to the floor: 'This isn't a third-class railway compartment!' Guaranteed to make me fighting mad, but I didn't mind. He was right. It was silly to play Philip Marlowe, Private Eye, when I was too shy to talk to a soul.

•

Things were going well at the radio. Alan Adair, an ex-B.B.C. announcer, took me aside and asked if I would like to join the staff: 'You're by far the best announcer we can afford'. . . . The head of the Newsroom also asked me to join him, said he'd always wanted to train up somebody who knew nothing whatsoever. While I was pondering these compliments, a telephone call came from my father. The Army was getting impatient, I was already overdue for call-up; was I going to stay abroad until I was twenty-eight which would give me exemption, or would I come back and do it? Up to me. I had to commit myself to ten years in Paris – but to go back was to throw away a lucky start – on the other hand I felt uneasy about dodging something everyone else had to do (perhaps I would always be lucky?) – I decided, reluctantly, to go back. I'd broken the thread of home all right,

and picked up another at once. Now, not for the last time,
I was throwing the new one away too.

The last night in Paris coincided with a party given by
some friends of Sturge's. I'd got the time wrong (my scrambled eggs scorned such petty details) and I hadn't eaten all
day. There was a kind of fruit-cup and I drank several glasses
of it quickly instead of supper in case some serious drinking
started later. Everyone appeared very glum, sipping their
mingy fruit-cup. I besought them to gaiety, replenished their
glasses; I'd expected my new friends to be more abandoned
than this.

A large fat girl I'd met once or twice in the little bar asked
me if I was all right. Of course I was. She suggested we take
a breath of air in the garden, and there I passed out.

Occasionally half-woken by brutal figures stealing my bed-
clothes (their coats the girl had pulled over me in the garden)
I truly woke up enveloped by the soft rise and fall of a very
large, sweet-smelling bosom. Unwilling to lose my first opportunity I made some exploratory movements, was gently
checked, and went back inside my nausea. We seemed to
be on a very narrow sofa in a dark room.

'Where am I?'

'Still here.'

A clock ticking inexorably somewhere in the house; the
last expiring coals collapsed in the grate.

'Where are the others?'

'Gone. I stayed to make sure you caught your train.'

My train. . . . So it was all over. I had to go back and be
a Boy Scout just when a bit of daylight was getting into my
head. Perhaps I could return, and they'd all still be here,
Sturge and the rest, Simon; I'd take my audition, write
poems. Dawn was coming through the window, fell on lip-
sticked glasses, spilling ash-trays, on a large earthenware
bowl the fruit-cup had come from.

'What was it?'

'White wine and gin.'

She got me back to Paris, to my train, where I passed out again. She got me to the Army. I don't even know if I thanked her, I never knew her name.

THE REST OF the intake came from Liverpool –
'I'm a Scouse Pa', what are you?' We sat in the freezing hut,
giving each other what cheer we could, while our details
were gone through by impatient men with stripes on their
arms. Then we were fallen-in and marched about, trailing
our feet, in a variety of clothing and hair-cuts (me in my
green corduroy jacket still unpaid for in Switzerland) feeling
new and conspicuous, cold and afraid. The Corporals who
marched at our side expressed despair at our appearance,
and mused theatrically about the stones we'd been found
under.

The Quarter-Master's Stores, the Regimental Barber's (O
my God!) and endless medical inspections and injections; the
next few days were spent naked, or nearly so, just waiting,
or queueing up, long past all pretence of being anything but
miserable and frightened, while Medical Officers and their
Orderlies fumbled with dirty syringes, smoked, and completely enclosed the distant stove.

'Bend over! Cough!' I saw the point of the old joke about
why we were called Privates; in fact we were called Troopers.
Knowing nothing about the Army and asked what I'd like

to be in, I'd remembered two friends in Switzerland who'd
gone into something called the 17/21st Lancers. That had the
right sort of ring about it, oblique stroke and all, so I'd put
my name down for them. Now I found myself a Trooper in
the Royal Tank Regiment which didn't sound quite the same
thing.

My jacket caused a grateful sensation among the N.C.O.s
and I could only bow my head and wait for the storm to
pass. Any rare leisure they allowed me ('our scruffy Artistic
Friend' was usually on cookhouse fatigues) I spent reading
Kafka in French, on my bed. I don't know why in French
except that Gallimard paper-backs had an exotic appeal for
me and I'd been reading this one in Paris. Anyway I probably
imagined Kafka had written it in French. My companions in
the barrack-room sternly silenced any intruder:

'Ssh! Pa's reading. Read us a bi', Pa'.'

'You gonna be an officer, Pa'?'

I couldn't imagine anything I'd like better than to let my
hair grow again, get out of filthy dungarees (mine always
smelled of a thousand greasy dishes), live in a nice warm
Mess like a golf clubhouse, and only come out occasionally
to lean on a stick and watch other people marching. I confessed this and they very much agreed, but we doubted my
chances. A corduroy jacket and being able to read French
were a start, but not much of one, I was so bad at everything
else.

I turned left when I should have turned right just half a
day after some of the others were getting the hang of it. I
wasn't the only one, but the instructors felt that in my case
I must be doing it deliberately. If my scrambled eggs were
serving me badly, it wasn't for want of trying. I'd surprised
myself by being very frightened indeed of the Regimental
Police, ex-jailbirds mostly, professional bullies. They seemed

to revive some half-buried memory of persecution. I knew if I got into their hands I'd have to defy them, for honour's sake, and so I'd never get away from them.

At weapon training, taking to pieces and re-assembling Bren-guns and so on, we competed. We began standing up and sat down as soon as we were finished. I was always the last left standing, my fingers are useless:

'Come on, you haven't got a house-maid to do your dirty work now!'

The boys from the other barrack-rooms would obediently snigger, but my friends prompted in whispers: 'No, the bolt, Pa'. No, the other way roun'.'

'For Gawd's sake! You'd find it quick enough if it had hair round it!'

That also was a false assumption.

•

One day all those who had passed School Certificate were commanded to fall out.

'This is it, Pa,' they whispered sadly, this was the break-up of the group. I had to go, it was all in my 'papers'. I'd been the stranger, they'd all known each other before, but they'd made me feel perfectly at home. And I was surprised at the warmth, something I'd never felt, not like that.

I was marched before three bluff senior officers and asked what school I'd been to and what my father did; and then they told me, without enthusiasm, that I would for the moment undergo special training as a 'Potential Officer' and move at once to the 'P.O. Block'.

I've often wished since I'd said 'No' and gone back to my friends; perhaps only because it would have been something to preen myself on. I can only admit it never occurred to me. Chiefly I wanted to get out of the eye of those infernal Policemen.

Once, swilling out the cookhouse late at night, I noticed

the rainbow colours of the scum caught in a little pocket in the concrete floor, iridescent under the electric lights. I was pushing it with my broom absent-mindedly, watching it shatter and reassemble, and heard a soft hiss in my ear: *'Jeeeesus Christ Almighty!!'* I looked up into a face puffy with bastardry, a Policeman on night-rounds, his tiny eyes for a moment at a loss. And then, very slowly: 'What's – your – name?' No need to make too much of this moment, but I'd been looking at those colours, and then into that face, from one to the other, and it told me more than I wanted to know.

.

I'd unwittingly fallen into one of the most highly disciplined regiments in the Army, and the most austere and windswept of camps, in the middle of winter. Catterick is on the Yorkshire moors, and on the highest and most exposed part of those moors there is a camp called by those outside it, with a touch of dread, the World's End. This was ours.

At the highest, windiest, most improbable point of World's End Camp, by itself (I'm sure all the other huts had long since blown away) stood the P.O. Block. Except that we lived in it, it was uninhabitable. There were cracks in the walls you could stick your hand through and get it bent by the gale outside. We slept in three or four layers of clothes, blankets on top of that, and on top of those kit-bags, steel-helmets, even rifles, anything to press the whole toppling mass down and prevent any pockets of air from forming. In the morning your nose, sticking above the surface like a schnorkel, throbbed with pain and blew out huge white clouds of steam, and within seconds of putting your fingers outside the blankets they'd lost all sensation and you groaned in spirit at the thought of the buckles that were to come.

As often as twice a week we had to produce all our equipment, laid out in a certain fashion, to be minutely examined first by the Sergeant and then by the Inca himself, Captain Ryder. This required staying up all night washing, ironing and polishing in a confined and irreducibly dirty space so that whatever you'd washed and ironed (itself a process of trial and error taking many hours) needed to be done again if you put it down anywhere, or if anyone brushed against it. The ingenuity of my companions astounded me, so did the zest and inventiveness they brought to this game.

Our beds had to be straight at the edges. With a mattress in three mis-shapen biscuit sections this was impossible, so they borrowed table tops from the NAAFI, wrapped their blankets around them and the result, not a straight bed at all but a table wrapped in blankets, seemed to me cheating. By the time I'd understood that this was an academic scruple they'd moved on to other spirited inventions – such as rolling their spare bootlaces like liquorice, tying them firm with black thread, and polishing them (both sides) until they lay like perfect commas on each side of the gleaming exclamation mark of the mess-tin. Mine, looking like what they were, spare bootlaces, were swept to the floor with the tip of Ryder's stick as though infected, together with the rest of the paraphernalia – spare vest PT, Full Service Marching Order, and so on, until a long night's work lay in a tangled heap round my stiffly-to-attention ankles and it had all to be done again for tomorrow. Another night without sleep.

What always surprised me was the lack of matiness, the way any of us who'd thought of a new dodge kept it to himself, though he knew the rest of us would suffer by comparison. It hadn't been like that in the other barrack-room. . . . I suppose it was right to collaborate so whole-heartedly with our oppressors since we were training to become one of their number. But I couldn't quite see it that way. Competition's the only thing that'll strike a spark out of some, just as you can teach dogs to slaver at the sound of a bell, but it's easy to learn to be crafty, and afterwards so difficult to forget.

.

A great part of each day was spent in what were called MT lessons (Motor Transport). These were of the *This-is-an-engine-so-called-because-it-drives* – *This-is-a-wheel-so-called-because-it-is-er-wheelshaped* variety, and were given us by Corporal Johnson, a man irresistibly doomed. He was breathless and fat and the world of physical objects was in a conspiracy to catch him out. Airily demonstrating the function of a particular nut he would give it a negligent twist, keeping his eye imperiously on us in order that we pay close attention, and it wouldn't budge. He'd push and push on the spanner, casually, concealing the effort, until he'd forget us, engage once again in the struggle that occupied his life; he'd put his knee into it, lie on his back and try it that way, calling out for another spanner by a technical name we didn't understand but which he could only repeat and repeat, embedded by this time in the machinery. In the end one of us would suggest it turned the other way, and flat on his back on the ground he'd stare up, incredulous at the fatuity of the suggestion, try it that way to prove his point, and of course it would turn, and he'd clamber to his feet, muttering to himself and the lesson went on, until the next booby-trap. Sometimes I laughed so much I couldn't pretend any more and sat gasping for breath, holding my stomach. He hated being laughed at, which made it all the more difficult to stop. In return he made me his butt – a fair arrangement.

It was also his duty to teach us to drive. The others knew how to, their fathers had cars, so after about three lessons on a lorry they were reasonably competent. I'd never sat in a driver's seat in my life and after three lessons I wasn't much wiser, with him at my side, squeaking, beating me over the head with a mess-tin.

'Old women of ninety' bash 'can drive' bash. 'So why the blankety' bash bash 'blank can't you!' I tried to point out he hadn't yet shown me how. 'Shurrup!' he'd scream and then, in a different register: 'Let's have tea-break.' The mess-tin came into use again, and we'd share it like conspirators. There was a sort of bond between us – he was without malice and he must have known there wasn't any in my laughter – I think he regarded me as part of the plot of the natural world to resist him, like a nut with a left-hand thread, or a swing-door that pushed the wrong way.

Unexpectedly I was called before the Squadron Leader; an unpleasant, pale man with spectacles, not seen before. 'Why are you here?' he snarled. (I'd been right about where that man at Butlin's had learned his manner.) I was obviously in some sort of trouble and remembering a tip of my brother's – always stare at a superior's cap-badge if you want to drive him mad, he can't quite tell whether you're looking at him or not – I did that and pretended to myself I wasn't frightened.

'You've been reported to me as having a flippant attitude towards the intricacies of the internal combustion engine!'

Corporal Johnson . . . only he could have invented such a phrase. He's ratted on me! Why didn't he warn me?

'I suppose you think that's clever!'

'No sir.' (I didn't.)

'Just because you've had an expensive education you imagine you're superior to N.C.O.s who are doing their job better than you'll ever do yours. You're a snob!'

A what? I'd never thought of it like that, I must say. And were you then only allowed to laugh at those who'd had an 'expensive education' also; patronise the rest perhaps?

'An officer! I wouldn't have you as a lance-corporal to hold open the door for me!' (Oh, so that's what you think of lance-corporals.) 'Get out!'

Corporal Johnson wasn't nearly so funny for any of us after that. He became subdued himself, almost respectful, as though he regretted the momentary exasperation that had made him go over to the enemy. It broke the spell, which was a pity because those lessons had taken place on a level of farce way outside the Army; they'd really begun to contain a kind of joy.

As it turned out he'd done me a good turn. When we went to Cadet School, after various other Boards and a wet week-end in Chester watched by vapid young men as we struggled to bridge a stream with a piece of string and half a plank, I found myself at the Infantry School at Eaton Hall, not the Cavalry one, near London. I was delighted because I'd taken a strong dislike to tanks.

Eaton Hall was, comparatively speaking, paradise. I started fiddling with pieces of cardboard, 'Squaring off' my spare socks, enquiring after the supply of NAAFI tables, and the others didn't know what I was talking about. It soon became clear that I'd been very unlucky in my Basic Training and that the worst was over.

It was February, we were a hundred miles further south and that strange house, like a dispirited Saint Pancras, had magnificent gardens that were beginning to stir. Even the constant early morning drill, stamping up and down, began to draw exhilaration from the spring.

The personalities of the Regimental Sergeant-Majors at the two National Service Cadet Schools acquired the status of legend among those who came across them. Indeed, after the pubs had closed at Oxford the hearties some-times fell in and marched each other back to college scream-ing '*Lafe* roy *lafe* roy' in loving imitation of their tones. This nostalgia for such a time, in such a place, was sad, and the noise they made horrible, but Regimental Sergeant-Major Copp had in fact, through the exercise of his profession, acquired characteristics that were notably less than human.

He had a face the colour of putty and so dramatically pocked it was as though it was stuck full of hollow-headed drawing-pins. His voice and vocal mannerisms bore hardly any relation to accepted human speech; his uniform was somewhere between an Officer's and an N.C.O.'s, an arcane military compromise that suggested a unique isolation. Indeed it was impossible to imagine him off-duty except in a Regimental Sergeant-Major's Mess of one, where he fed on failed cadets perhaps, cooked by breathing at them, wearing his hat because it was riveted on. He stood each day in front of six hundred boys, worn by his uniform rather than wearing it; first he'd thunderously hope we'd all had a 'damn good rear' (for some reason) and then he'd start letting out this curious non-human bark until eventually his sole purpose was achieved and we moved (our limbs) as one boy. As an exercise in concentration and exclusiveness it was effective, frightening and completely ridiculous.

I only saw him once close-to and the lack of expression in his vast head startled me. On that occasion he simply looked me up and down with colourless boiled eyes and muttered in a hoarse croak that I wasn't a front-rank soldier, never would be, and so with much shrilling and clicking from his minion Sergeant-Majors and Guards Corporals I was removed, grateful, to the comparative obscurity of the centre file.

There was only one thing genuinely to fear at Eaton Hall and that was the Adjutant's inspection. It didn't often happen, depending on his God-like whim, but if he found any fault with you it meant a period in the cells. I have a dread of confinement and every morning parade looked anxiously, so did we all, towards the steps of the Officers' Mess in the far corner of the barrack square, to see if that elegant figure in his batman-shone riding boots was slowly descending, carefully wiping the last of his breakfast egg from his close-shaven mouth. It never happened. It looked as if he'd forgotten us, or mellowed.

One week-end I went away for forty-eight hours' leave and returned just in time for early morning parade. I hadn't shaved, or cleaned my equipment, but during that forty-eight hours I'd contrived to forget about such things; I only remembered the enormity of it as I ran on to the parade ground. However, sometimes we weren't inspected at all; the only danger was that the Adjutant would choose this morning to come out. He did.

The way these things are done in the Army, and in this case the *dramatis personae* were hand picked, takes the form of a primitive drama of propitiation and retribution. The Adjutant slowly, negligently enters from the guessed-at luxuries of the palace. The Regimental Sergeant-Major, Court Chamberlain to his Crown Prince, pretends not to notice him, just puts more resonance into his bark, dredges up hitherto reserved expressions of exasperation and threat. The Officer waits at a distance, suggesting by his absentminded stance that he is condescending to watch, but not closely, because what he sees is distasteful to his refinement. This continues for a few moments until dread has really mounted in those who are being paraded and then the R.S.M., the moment perfectly chosen, sees him; with stamps and turns that make the tarmacadam sound hollow he marches towards him so fast it seems he'll never pull up in time. He does however, with a crescendo bang, and salutes as though trying to snap his arm off at the elbow. The object of his veneration raises his own hand to his cap with infinite care, murmurs a formula, the R.S.M. marches back to a position in front of the parade, turns to face it, pauses for effect, and then screams with a volume obviously kept in store for just such a scene:

'Atten-Shun!' He then mutters commands in a pretence of *sotto voce* to his subordinates, and these contain terror, his terror, at the visitation that is about to befall the rest of us. The Company Sergeant-Majors pass on this terror to the Corporals who immediately begin pulling at us, bashing at our rifles, ostentatiously putting us to rights. Now, all is prepared.

The Adjutant strolls along the ranks, ostensibly very bored, pausing occasionally, flipping with his index finger a buckle or a rifle-sling, never quite looking at it, not saying a word, like a fantasy poet correcting his proofs, attended by an adoring cortège of compositors. His merest gesture is enough: 'Sarnt Majah, take that gentleman's name!' A stomach-turning rumble from the heart of the putty-coloured volcano. The C.S.M. addressed flurries with self-conscious haste to the offender, muttering darkly, meanwhile the Adjutant has passed on, still silent, as though this plebeian system of crime and punishment has nothing to do with him. His whole dignity and effectiveness, and by this time these are enormous, depend entirely on the supporting players. The more they roar and stamp the more he can slouch, the more Olympian and detached he can appear. The caste above is being created, with diligence, by the caste below.

These reflections did not occupy me at the time. In military terms I was treasonably filthy; for just one of the dirtinesses, my unshaven chin for instance, I could get three or four days, and for that one I had twenty more – they'd throw away the key. The Adjutant and his entourage worked their way slowly towards me. I thought seriously of making a dash for it, finding a ship. . . . I felt rather than heard my own Company Sergeant-Major go very still behind me.

'Ker-rist-all-bloody-mighty! You are a dozy bugger, sir, and no fucking mistake!'

I'd never heard him swear before, it was against their code

apparently, they managed to curse blood-curdlingly without it; but now he was talking in his normal voice, almost to himself, lost in wonder at the sight of me.

'Faint!'

I didn't understand at first. He came back again behind me and hissed in my ear: 'Faint! For God almighty's sake FAINT!' Obediently I buckled at the knees.

'Fall in two men either side! You! Take his rifle.' The roar was simultaneous with my knees bending and I was marched back by my two delighted flanking companions to the safety of the barracks; we'd escaped.

I saw the Company Sergeant-Major afterwards and he just shook his head from side to side as if to say survival is the first law and you haven't even sense enough for that.

.

In one respect at least I was well organised. Just outside the grounds of Eaton Hall there was a pub, and the owner had a very pretty, very shy daughter, whom I liked very much. We all went there in the evenings and soon, however broke I might be, there was a pint of beer drawn into my special pewter mug, and a packet of cigarettes. My pay we spent together in Chester, the rest of the week I was discreetly on the house.

Sometimes after closing time she could escape and we walked through the gardens in the soft spring and early summer evenings, along the rhododendron alleys by the lakes and I'd read to her, or talk, or we'd just sit together. She was seventeen and I was nineteen and I owe her much. During the day, my ear cocked for the poem that always seemed somewhere about but never quite arrived, I drifted incompetently through a world that became more and more incomprehensible. Scrambling out of one pitfall after another I wouldn't take precautions to avoid the next one because I'd no hard centre I could trust; I felt I might become what

I pretended. In a society as cut and dried as the Army, as basically simple, this was disastrous. But in the evenings there was Rita, her fondness for me, and her understanding. With her I felt I grew back to my proper shape; the world that I insisted was real seemed to become so, and we lived in it together.

·

Our chief instructor was an elegant, withdrawn Captain in the Rifle Brigade with the splendid surname of Pontifex. He was also remarkable for his patience.

As a boy in Wales I'd led gangs over the hills, engaged in thrilling battles with pine-cones, attack, counter-attack, encirclement and so on; platoon tactics are exactly the same. But in the Army everything is reduced to a drill, practised over and over again so that if you lose your head you're likely to do the right thing out of habit. The sequence – Reconnaissance, Plan, Method, etc. – was even printed on a card, and no other was allowed. Something very odd happened to my brain; I couldn't learn it. Child's play reduced to a formula and I couldn't get it into my head. I completely lost my nerve and became a sort of idiot. After one long day in the hills, my mind having turned completely to mush, every question answered totally, hopelessly wrong, we turned and marched homeward. Pontifex halted us on the brow of a hill and in a tired, gentle voice, giving me a last chance to get something right, asked me to show the direction we'd just come from. Miserably I stabbed my finger, blind, into the air; sadly he shook his head, sighed, and we continued, all of us silent, on our march.

At our periodical interviews Pontifex would ask me, in so many words, what was the matter? I could be so good at some things, but at others. . . . As for my grading . . . we were graded, like eggs, and he was much too gentle a man ever to tell me how near to a reject I must have been. 'And

why,' he once asked, closing his eyes, a spasm of pain cross-
ing his face, 'why do you wear that extraordinary jacket?'

Somehow I survived and we came to the Passing Out
Dinner. I was elected to sit next to Pontifex because it was
thought I might amuse him. Flattering, but I doubted it,
guessed he might have had his fill of me by now. However,
so it was arranged and on the great night we solemnly sat
round a horse-shoe table while the waiters called us sir. In
the centre was the Company Commander, a man about
whom I knew nothing except he had an eccentric taste in
military hats, and the top cadets were on either side of him.
I sat at the bottom of one of the legs of the horse-shoe with
Pontifex on my right. He was clad in the full bottle-green
Number Ones of the Rifle Brigade, a thick patent leather
bandolier across his chest with a huge silver plaque in the
middle; intimation of the glories we were heir to. We were
now his brother officers and he seemed weighed down, even
for him, by an unusual burden of sadness; perhaps it was
the weight of the bandolier. He only addressed me twice in
the course of the evening. The first time was to remind me,
with infinite melancholy, that the port always passed to the
left. When it came to the port, having no one on my left,
and no one in front of me, I passed it back to him. With the
pent-up vexation of four months, though still controlled, he
spoke to me for the last time.

'Oh, Kavanagh, Kavanagh! You'll learn, you'll learn!'

Unless I'd stood up and turned my back on the room and
passed the decanter across my body I don't know what else
I could have done. I expect there's an answer.

I'D PUT MY NAME down for the Royal Innis-killing Fusiliers because they sounded an Irish regiment and because they were stationed in Jamaica. To my delight I was indeed commissioned into that Regiment (usually only the more successful cadets were given their first choice) but was dashed to find myself posted, not to the West Indies, but to the North Irish Brigade Training Depot, Ballykinler, County Down.

In a brand-new officer's caubeen, a sort of floppy blue bonnet with a grey cockade of feathers sticking out of it, a black-thorn stick in one hand and a civilian-looking suitcase in the other, I reported to the Officers' Mess.

It was as ridiculously comfortable as I'd hoped. White-coated waiters showed me to my room and I was given a batman. He was a wily little man in an open-necked shirt who wore his plimsolls, as well he might, like a badge of triumph. To be Excused Boots in the Army is to escape all the less pleasant parts of army life and is extremely difficult. It takes real ingenuity to con the Medical Officer into granting the magic formula. I admired him at once.

The other second-lieutenants, all transmogrified like myself from recruits to cadets to Northern Ireland, were pleasant and friendly. One took me aside and asked if I was queer. I suppose he thought I might help to pass the time and I was sorry to disappoint him, but he took it philosophically.

Passing the time was indeed the problem. Newly joined recruits came here for their Basic Training, were put through the same paces as I had been a few months before, although much less arduously, and we were meant to supervise. How best to do this I never discovered. I tried leaning on my stick and just watching, but apart from the fact that people marching up and down is a spectacle of limited interest, I felt my own idleness was becoming conspicuous and hurried off elsewhere, also to watch; it was all we were allowed to do. The training sergeants knew their simple business backwards, and the bad ones were too set in their ways to take suggestions. Anyway I felt that to stand about watching when they were doing the instructing was a kind of insult, and distracted the recruits. I'd no desire to make life difficult for anyone, least of all myself, and within a few weeks the boredom was insupportable.

Ballykinler is on a sandy, duny coast near the Mountains of Mourne – where they put the prisoners after Easter 1916. I suppose, now, I might find it beautiful. But in those days life was busy not living up to what was expected of it, and the Mountains of Mourne were grey heaps of slag, the sands stretched drearily away into a monotonous infinity, and it was always raining. I used sometimes to walk in the evening with Patrick Sarsfield along the yellow sands, both of us in our different ways inveighing against our fate. He was older than I was, had been to Oxford, and was much better educated. He could talk wittily and excitingly about authors I'd only heard of, and some I hadn't, and his main hatred and despair were reserved for the philistinism and coarseness of the other officers in the mess.

I felt rather guilty talking to him about this because although everything he said was true, I liked them very much. I enjoyed Mess Nights with their formality – 'Gentlemen, The King' – lots to eat and drink and the Pipe Major and his Corporal marching round and round the tables playing the bagpipes until you were quite drunk with the deafening, stirring noise and were banging the table and shouting with the rest; and then ritual heartiness and rough games afterwards. I liked the crazy Irish dancing classes with a lot of sweating middle-aged men all holding hands in the 'Haymaker's Jig' while the Pipe Major solemnly put us right: 'No, to the left now, Colonel, to the left.' 'Oh, bless my soul! Thank you Pipe Major,' puff puff, 'thank you!' I enjoyed their unsuspicious good manners, the way it was taken for granted you were a good chap until you proved otherwise; their genuine concern for their men, and the easy relationship they had with their N.C.O.s, which may have been feudal, but to my eyes at least was so delicately balanced inside the existing framework as to be as nearly as possible just. They were mostly Irish, Northern and Southern, and this may have had something to do with it, but I have no reason to think an English regiment is much different. In fact, to my shame, for I felt that a poet, even one who hadn't written a decent poem, should have hated all their easy assumptions, I found there were aspects of army life, its simplicity chiefly, that I enjoyed and admired. There remained, however, the boredom.

•

My Company Commander was known to everyone, behind his back, as 'Crackers', and among his many claims to that title was his incapacity, amounting to frenzy, to understand anything but the appearance of extreme busyness. This was hard to keep up for the whole of a long empty day. He could stride about purposefully, on mysterious errands of his own, communing with himself; but it wasn't so easy for the rest of us.

As we weren't allowed into the Mess during 'working' hours, I'd taken to hiding in the dunes with a book. One day I looked up to see Crackers staring down at me with an expression of fascinated horror. Heaven knows what he was doing there. He didn't say a word but backed away, still staring at me, remounted his bicycle and wobbled off. From that time on he treated me with a sort of watchful deference as though one false move from me and he'd scream the place down. Often I looked up to find his eyes fixed on me with that same expression of creepy horror.

Otherwise I kept reasonably out of trouble, except when I overslept as duty officer and had to hand over the keys of the Guardroom in my pyjamas. I was marched in front of the Colonel for that and given seven extra days as duty-officer. (No one could convince Crackers I hadn't thought that was the *correct* way to hand-over. He just nodded his head looking more and more frightened. . . .) This punishment was the officer-equivalent of confined to barracks, slightly harder work because it meant loss of sleep. What I hated most about it was visiting the prisoners. The Police, accomplices now, threw open the door of each cell with a grinding clank and screamed at a man four feet away: 'Stand by your bed!' and you had to ask if there were any complaints and always staring straight in front of him, or at the floor, he said: 'No'.

I talked about this farce in the Mess and was of course told not to be sentimental, they were all 'hard cases', etc. They were indeed, I think, but to set professional bullies to knock the stuffing out of hard cases was wasteful and dishonest. There was a pleasant feeling of 'us-ness' in the unit. Were the prisoners 'us' or had they comfortably become 'them'?

Two or three times I sat on a court-martial as 'Officer under instruction'. The three officers of the Court, amiable, lazy men, would always decide Guilty and chat of this and that while one of them looked up the maximum punishment permissible. They'd ask my opinion and I'd mumble something about maybe it wasn't him, or extenuating circumstances and so on, and they'd smile and push over his record, and sure enough there was the long list of petty crimes and desertions sometimes stretching back for years. But was there any use in sending this frightened creature for another spell in probably the most horrible prison in Britain? Why not kick him out of the Army altogether? That would mean a district court-martial, a big affair, and Colonels got a bad name if they referred too many internal cases to the Generals. So really he was being condemned out of loyalty to the Colonel; because it was expedient. These men, nice men, certainly had no ability to imagine what they were doing. I could imagine, that was what I was good at, but I couldn't do anything. These verses I made up all day long in my head, even if I wrote them down, what would they ever change? How was it ever possible to get through to Them?

•

Towards the end of my extra spell as duty-officer, one Saturday when all the others had gone away for the weekend and I sat alone in the Mess reading back-numbers of the Regimental magazine 'Faugh a ballagh', the Mess waiter came with an urgent summons from Crackers. I walked over the empty parade ground in the rain, to his bungalow at the edge of it, and found him sitting, staring in front of him, fiercely stroking his cross-eyed Siamese.

'Terrible . . . terrible,' he sighed.

'The responsibility! . . . terrible . . . tomorrow . . . the only officer in the camp. . . . You!

'I've held on as long as I could, but tomorrow I must go

out; tomorrow; have to.' He began to pace the room, the Siamese dangling furiously from his hand.

'Captain Cowan . . . massing! The Irish Republican Army. . . . Time for their Spring Offensive! Can you Hold the Fort?'

It seemed unlikely to me that Captain Cowan, whoever he might be, was waiting for Crackers to go out for the afternoon before he swooped on the Camp, but I put on as martial an air as I could and Crackers laid his hand on my shoulder, staring into my eyes, Ronald Colman on the North-West Frontier. He'd stayed behind as long as he could, but now it was Goodbye, my boy . . . God bless you!

I'd seen Southern Ireland for the first time a few weeks before. We'd gone for a ride in a Naval destroyer and I'd peered from the deck at the low blue coast of Donegal, shrouded in rain, and thought of my forefathers, of all the songs, and the stories I'd heard since I was a child and how I'd always felt it was there I belonged.

Captain Cowan, perhaps guessing that Crackers was expected to return, held his hand.

•

A few days later my father wrote, asking me to join him in Dublin. I had some leave due and in a great state of excitement – visiting my country at last! – I set out to cross the fabled border.

The train from Belfast was disappointingly ordinary. I'd been given a First Class rail warrant and sat in the restaurant car, dressed in my officer-type Prince of Wales check (I'd regretfully abandoned the struggle between the Army and my green corduroy jacket) drinking whisky, allowing the deferential dining-car attendants to wait on me in the manner to which, during the past month or two, I'd become fairly accustomed. When we crossed the border I stared at the landscape of my race; subtly different, it seemed to me. The train itself seemed different, the dining-car staff had changed

– and now there was a figure standing behind me – the Head Attendant looking doubtful.

'Would you be Pat Kavanagh?' I said I would.

'How's it going then? I'm Joe Lyons. Have a drink.' And he threw himself into the seat beside me.

'I'd tell that look anywhere. I was having a drink with your father and Jimmy, and they told me to look out for you.'

And he'd recognised me – Prince of Wales check notwithstanding. I felt I was coming home.

So my father was with Jimmy O'Dea, the marvellous comedian, almost a legend. I'd last seen him in Llanfairfechan in North Wales when I was eleven. He used to come to us from Ireland with packets of tea and sugar sewn into his clothes so he could hardly walk off the boat, and bring with him a suggestion of lights allowed to burn after dark, and of unrationing, that I scarcely remembered. One Sunday we'd all gone to Mass together on the sea-front of that gloomy little granite-and-slate resort. It was said by an aged Franciscan with a white beard like Santa Claus and a red motor-bike, and it took place in the Amusement Arcade. Before Mass he heard confessions behind the counter of the Rifle Range, underneath a notice that said *The Attendant's Decision Is Final*. It was Jimmy who pointed this out to me, his handkerchief stuffed into his mouth, crying with laughter: it was the first time I'd been let in on a grown-up joke and I adored him for it.

In Dublin, where my father was being treated *en prince*, there was a flurry of friends and conspiratorial nods and winks and 'arrangements' that I guessed bewildered him as much as they did me. Joe Lyons, it turned out, was a key man in this respect, and could get things that otherwise were unobtainable. This was puzzling, because there didn't seem to be any kind of shortage. Noel Purcell, the Irish actor, bearded like an Old Testament prophet, was especially good at instilling drama into the simplest occasion. Once, about six o'clock in the evening, well within licensing hours anyway, he tipped his huge, sombrero-like hat to the back of his head, leaned across to my father and whispered behind his hand: 'What'll you have?' My father, startled, suggested a gin and tonic. Raising the hand as who should say 'It shall be done', he slowly dropped his lids over his eyes and with a barely perceptible movement of his head called a waiter to his side:

'Tom . . . three gins and tonics for my Friends,' emphasising the last word meaningfully – 'and' he laid a detaining hand on the waiter's arm – 'good ones, mind!' The waiter winked in reply and strolled away, pausing to chat with other drinkers on his way across the room. After a decent interval, say half an hour or so, he returned – with three gins and tonics.

Later that evening we went with Jimmy to the Catholic Stage Guild which was said to be the only place you could get a decent drink at that hour. (It was still very early, but never mind.) It was of course shut, but after a conversation whispered into an area we were, equally of course, let in, shown to a little cellar where there was a bar, and left to ourselves. I was elected barman, told the price of whisky, climbed over the bar and got busy, delighted at the way the evening was turning out, and to be with my father and an old friend. After a while there were murmurs and thumpings upstairs and the little man who'd let us in came scampering down calling out that the O'Reilly brothers had arrived, and others, and he'd tried to say he was closed but they'd heard talking and he didn't like the look of it but he'd done his best. By this time they were there and the tiny cellar was filled to bursting.

Soon their bill began to mount, but when it came to paying

they never actually did. If I didn't hear a complicated order they'd say: 'Deaf or something?' taking me for a professional barman, and I was interested to learn what a professional barman is expected to put up with. It seemed churlish to nag them, but I felt a glow of responsibility and kept a careful tally. When it got to five pounds I reminded the larger and more commanding of the O'Reillys and he surprised me by saying: 'So what?' not at all politely.

'I'd like the money, please.'

'Oo yew wud wud yew?'

Doing a very incompetent imitation of my accent he turned his back. Someone, I think it was Jimmy, tipped me the wink to be careful, they were ex-Palestine Policemen, and terrors in drink.

I wasn't going to have my good-humour spoiled by ex-Palestine Policemen, so I held my peace until he came back for another vast order. This I politely withheld until he paid what he owed, on the grounds that I was losing count, which I was.

There was suddenly dead silence in the bar; the other brother lurched across and they both stared at me, the green-horn barkeep in the ol' saloon:

'What did you say?'

I said what I'd said.

'You snotty-nosed little English . . .'

A woman crawled under the bar and scratched at my ankles:

'For the love of God don't start anything,' she whispered in great terror. 'They mean no harm. It'll be all right.'

'I just want the money.'

'Come out and fight us.'

'I'd prefer to do it one at a time.'

(One is seldom at one's best in such exchanges.)

'Oo, nervous are we, our little ickey-bickey mother's boy?'

and he leaned across the bar and flicked out my tie. Not being a professional barman and having no job to lose, I jumped over the bar and hit him. I put into it all my hatred of Them, of the Police, Regimental and Palestine, and my feeling for Ireland which men like these drag down, and it did me good. Immediately one of the brothers came up behind me and pinioned my arms so the other could bash me unimpeded – they must have been a great success in the Palestine Police – but Jimmy danced in between, laughing and pleading. The women were crying out and holding on to the men, and altogether it was an animated scene. Then came the clatter of many large feet from upstairs, and among curses and threats of vengeance, the bar was cleared and we were left to ourselves.

'They would have murdered you. They would have stamped on your face and then burst into tears and sworn they hadn't meant it.'

My father was very shaken. The manager came down in despair. 'They're not even Members. They'll never cross the door again.'

Jimmy made all reasonably smooth and I walked back to the hotel with my father. We sat drinking together till late. 'You must be more careful,' he kept saying, but I knew he hadn't liked the O'Reillys any more than I had. I'd struck my blow, but we both wished my first evening in Ireland hadn't been like that.

·

National Service was increased from eighteen months to two years – suddenly I was less than half-way through; it became important to find some way of getting out of Ballykinler – not easy, hardly anyone really liked being there.

All the Regular Officers spoke longingly of battalion life. There you had your own platoon, or company, the faces were familiar and remained the same – it was like a family

– real soldiering! This sounded better than the Boy Scout business of leaning on a stick while the stream of bewildered recruits washed past you through the camp, but the battalion was full up, and anyway had no enthusiasm for unfamiliar, National Service faces.

The war in Korea had broken out and the Royal Ulster Rifles, in the East already, were warned to stand by. This was a loophole, transfer within the Irish Brigade was relatively easy. I talked it over with Patrick Sarsfield, and we volunteered. But they didn't want National Servicemen in Korea either, only Regulars and Reservists, so that was that.

After the initial slaughter of American conscripts there was a lull; the fighting started up again; the Rifles went into the line, had casualties, and the Adjutant asked us if we still wanted to go, it looked a nasty business? We were given embarkation leave.

We reported to a camp called, exotically, J/RHU. This stood for Japan/Reinforcement Holding Unit, so the battalion was still elusive, but Japan sounded attractive enough.

We were the only National Servicemen; the rest were Regulars and Reservists. These last were very unfortunate men. Some of them had gone right through the 39–45 war and had just about made the transition to normal life when they were recalled. They thought they'd done with the Army for good, but now, because of an unlucky position on the list, or a specialist skill, their lives were in little pieces again; their wives now had to make do on allowances, or what their husbands could save – there were mortgages to pay off, small businesses started, and so on; no guarantee their jobs would be there when they got back, this was no glamorous patriotic struggle, the public hardly knew it was going on – *if* they got back. No wonder they looked worried and filled the Mess with the noise of scratching pens as they tried to reassure their wives.

Others of the Reservists frankly gloried in it. Immediately they set about the cultivation of huge moustaches, and when they could wore revolvers, slap slap against a well-pressed thigh. At the local pub they had their names engraved on pewter mugs to be collected when they returned – *if* they returned, they were not above hinting darkly – causing a wetness in the barmaid's eye. After closing time they rolled back to the Mess and bawled choruses of dirty songs, always the same choruses and always the simpler, more straight-forward ones, and at the best bits they laughed on cue so much that sometimes they were sick on the carpet. One evening Patrick and I came back from Leeds and found them unconscious, in various attitudes of slumber, all over the Mess. One of them was peeing while he slept, it dribbled out of the end of his darkened trouser-leg on to the floor.

'Who on earth do these men marry?' I wondered.

'Their sisters!' said Patrick, but I didn't believe him. I couldn't imagine these hairy songsters had their female equivalents.

Everyone was a 'shadow' Adjutant or Quarter-Master or Colonel, ready to take over when necessary. We were just spares like the Regular subalterns and the soldiers. But al-ready eyes were on Patrick. His nervous distaste for any kind of disorder or stupidity drew him inevitably, against his will, to the headquarters office. There he would go through ac-cumulated piles of paper with sharp whinnies of disgust, until he had reduced them to sense and was, within days, one of the two or three people in the camp who knew about the running of it.

He drew me up a reading list for the voyage. Admiring his erudition as I did, even I was startled when he chose the complete prose works of Milton as his companion for the next eight weeks at sea. I settled for *Ulysses* and soon the great day came.

POOP! POOP! went the funnels of the big boat and slowly, crabwise, it slid away from the grey wharves of Liverpool, greasy in the rain. Gratefully we turned to explore the Officers' bar. This was a kind of deck-house with windows, furnished in old leather like a West End club, and there we received our first drinks, shipboard-size at shipboard prices, from the hands of an attentive steward. I settled myself with my huge drink into an equally huge armchair, while the rain tore at the windows, and prepared to enjoy being borne, at the Army's expense, to the mysterious East.

There was a worm in the Garden of Eden. On board there were only two classes: luxury and sub-steerage. We were crammed six in a cabin admittedly, but we had the bar and the spaces of the upper deck. The soldiers, the 'men', of whom there were a great number, ate and slept on a Mess Deck which was in fact a hold, with hardly any ventilation, and to climb down to see them during the night as Duty Officer was to drop into a stinking pit. During the day they were not much better off. There was hardly any room on the afterdecks; these were littered with all the usual knobbly ship's furniture and they squatted on the awkward hatch-covers, or between the lifeboat derricks, a dense mass of khaki bodies. They weren't allowed to drink, but they had the pleasure of watching us, sprawled in old-fashioned P. and O. deck-chairs, enjoying our long, misted glasses.

Some of the older officers, the Regulars, and those Reservists whose own problems were most pressing, occupied themselves with the Mess Decks, trying to pass on what they'd learned about their own positions. Many of the recalled soldiers had left their families in hardship – morale was not high. None of us had any clear idea what this war was about and most of us had clung to the hope that it would be over before we got there. Everyone except the bawdy-songsters and myself. I was in search of experience without bothering much what kind. I suppose they were too.

I didn't see much of Patrick on the voyage. He was more and more concerned with administration whereas I did nothing but read and drink; I think my irresponsibility annoyed him. I shared a cabin with two Reservists and three straight-backed boys from Sandhurst who were gentle and simple and intelligent. They belonged to the pre-1914 world rather than to mine and, sure enough, two of them were decorated and all of them were killed.

.

Our first stop was Port Said, and my first sight of it, postponed until the others had rushed on deck, was through a port-hole crept up to sideways. I wanted to take the Near East by surprise. I saw, Oh glory! a red fez, a palm-tree, and a patch of white sand. I went up on deck. The ugly town, its Derry & Toms architecture coloured by the astonishing light – a corny picture-postcard, exactly as I'd imagined it. But this familiarity was the greatest surprise.

We wandered into the flaking, French-Oriental streets: 'Hey! MacTavish! Buy my sister?' 'Hey, MacTavish! Buy a battle-ship?' It was a game – they enjoyed playing it. Gully-gully men surrounded us; I allowed one to do what he wanted; he produced three fluffy ducklings from my trouser pocket together with my change, and vanished. 'Hey! MacTavish! Genuine Spanish Fly?' We scoured the book-shops for pornography, which so far as we could read among the misprints was always about monks, extravagantly endowed underneath their habits, making lengthy and repetitive entries into swooning nuns. Knowing something about monks and nuns, these were not among my fantasies. We tried to buy dirty postcards, with no success; even the likeliest, shiftiest-looking vendor sounded hurt: 'No, sir! No good sir! King Farouk very clean man!'

We finished up at a night-club which we hoped might contain the heights of wickedness. Instead there were henna'd French ladies old enough to be our mothers and a decorous Victor Sylvester-type band. We danced obediently with our partners, trying not to notice their false-teeth, as they ground their pelvic bones so painfully into us; they too felt false, padded out with some hard substance such as teak.

·

The ship was surrounded by bum-boats, filled with fruit and carpets and unidentifiable leather objects with pictures of the Sphinx on them in red and blue, and in the boats grinning, friendly Egyptians, calling out.

Bargaining was done from the deck, the purchase fastened to a rope, the money attached to the rope and hauled down. Just as we were beginning to move, an argument broke out in the boats, something hadn't been paid for. The Egyptian was appealing, smiling hopefully up. Someone threw an enamel tea-mug down at him. The aim was perfect, it struck him in the middle of his face and split it across; he collapsed in the bottom of his little boat, a mask of blood; we sailed away.

After Suez the Red Sea; Biblical mountains in unfiltered sun, again like objects remembered. Sleeping on deck you could measure the slow roll of the boat by watching the Pleiades sway to either side of the rigging, and feel the inaudible turbines throbbing in your back, the soft air on your face, warm as milk. About five in the morning the Lascar crew hosed down the deck and I grabbed my blanket before they hosed me, in a dawn of incredible pinks and greens, fleeing from the sun down to the cabin below.

At Rimbaud's Aden, that dreadful pile of ash where nothing natural grows or lives, we stopped just long enough for damage to be done to property and girls; someone had to pay for the soldiers being cooped up like that.

By Singapore I'd decided things weren't going at all to plan. I'd made no kind of contact with the East. When we stopped we went ashore full of idiotic hopes, awkward officers on shore-leave, shook off the touts, wandered about pretending to have a marvellous time and then finished up somewhere like the Grand Orient Hotel drinking expensive English drinks and reading the airmail edition of *The Times*. At least the soldiers got drunk and had to be carried up the gang-plank by their friends. We spent the days until the next stop in lying boasts about adventures had in the last one. The bawdy songsters were particularly good at this, but once ashore they seemed to shrink, and clung to each other; it was only back on board they retrieved their full broth-of-a-boyishness.

I felt something had to be made happen so I went ashore alone which was against the rules and told a rickshaw driver to take me out of bounds, to a girl. Not very inventive – a little in the bawdy-songsters' line perhaps – but it seemed the obvious way to start. He set off, very fast. Pavements gave way to pitted asphalt, and that turned into a mud-track; stone houses became shacks and then there was nothing but low huts, the only lights little braziers surrounded by dark squatting figures. I tried to make him turn back (servicemen were murdered here every day of the week) but he didn't seem to hear – panted on up alleys, down cartways until we were past the scurfy fringes of the town. There he stopped and I was greeted in the dark roadway by a dreadful painted woman of about seventy with gold teeth. She pushed aside the bead curtain of her shack and by the light of a taper showed me a mud-floored room with five or six girls astraddle an open drain that ran through the middle of it, douching themselves. I stuck my head in and pulled it out again quickly and madam wanted to know why, becoming angry; the girls came out, adding their cries; male figures appeared from the dark and one of them grabbed the back of my green corduroy jacket (incognito donned for the expedition). I took what money I had on me (not much, I wasn't that green), distributed it quickly, mumbling apologies, and while they were trying to see how much it was ducked through the group and ran off down the dark alley. I guessed the rickshaw driver would hang around for his cut and at last I found him, asleep between the wheels. I jumped in and pointed at the distant lights of the city, shouting. We were surrounded again, they were grabbing me and he appeared to hesitate: summoning every ounce of the British raj within me I shouted and shouted until Queen Victoria herself must have heard, and reluctantly he trotted me away. I was ashamed I'd had to do this, for all I knew they were telling me of a better place to go; but that isn't what it sounded like and I was more relieved than ashamed.

The first sight of Japan was through the dark; in the morning we found hills all around us, coming down sharply to the windows, perfect triangles neatly layered with rice-fields, the apex green with fir trees to the tip; an old Australian barracks left over from the 1945 occupation. It was nearly Christmas and we were welcomed with many parties – American, Australian, New Zealand – we were the first British to arrive since the end of the war. There were nurses too waiting for fresh wounded; these hadn't been provided yet, the war was at stale-mate. Christmas Day I spent under close arrest for assaulting a superior officer. He'd been troublesome at an Australian party and in the accents of Godalming had besought me, 'a fellow Paddy', to show these Australian bastards what we could do; the Irish name of his Regiment had obviously gone to his head. Largely for his own good (I think) and before he could get really hurt, I tried to knock him out in the lavatory, which proved more difficult than it looks on the films. In hospital he'd mentioned my name and I was arrested. After a while the Australians explained that I'd acted out of politeness and I was released, only to be called in front of the Colonel again. The day before I'd been found by one of the senior nurses in the Nurses' Mess with one of the junior ones and for this the Colonel, bored with the senior nurse and bored with me, gave me my second spell of extra orderly-officer. Most of it I spent hoping too many of my Regiment would not come back in the middle of the night under Australian police escort, dripping blood. The Irish didn't seem to like the Australians, but they were outnumbered.

Apart from the parties, life was much the same as it had been in Ireland. I was leaning on my stick again, but now my hat was pulled over my eyes, because of hangover. Japan was useless, this fascinating country that we were cut off from because we had to wear uniform all the time, were in effect part of an army of occupation, which is no way to get to understand anywhere. Once again, somehow, nothing was *happening* to me. I did all I could to reach Korea, tried everything, but it was no use, there wasn't room. There'd been no fighting for ages, nobody needed to be replaced.

Colonel (Mad Mike) Llewellyn came out from England to give us battle-practice. We stood on freezing hill-tops while he told us how to hit them where it hurts, screaming a little, his head wagging from side to side fervently, the snot falling out of his nose, blown like streamers in the wind. He gave us bayonet practice, encouraging us with semi-voluntary grunts and gargles that made him dribble from the mouth as well as the nose.

About this time I heard of a military P.R.O. set-up, Public Relations Officers who looked after journalists in Korea. At least it was a way of getting there; I could go and see the battalion and perhaps they might let me join them. It was worth a try and after a few balked attempts I got to the man in charge. We baffled each other about equally I think, but he promised vaguely 'to let me know'.

Patrick was a bigwig at Headquarters by now and wangled me a trip to Tokyo as a courier, the first time I'd been able to get away from the barracks. It involved travelling by night, delivering whatever it was, and coming back the next night. The train was full of hospitable Americans armed with hip-flasks, so the night passed agreeably enough; the day not so well after a night like that, and coming back there were more Americans similarly equipped, and to carry on where you'd left off seemed the only way to keep your head on. Back at the barracks I had two nights' sleep to catch up with, but I was urgently summoned to the Adjutant. I'd been posted to Korea as a 'War Office Observer' and was to leave at once.

It took a day in a lorry to reach the airfield and my brain felt it had come loose in my head; I wondered if I had alcoholic poisoning. About nine we arrived; I was shown a bunk, the first I'd seen for sixty hours, and told I left at dawn. An elderly Major stood looking at me as I stood look-ing at the bunk. 'Come and have a drink!'

'No thank you.'

'My jeep's waiting!' It was an order. He marched off.

After about an hour in the bar I tried to leave. It was a

two-mile walk across the tarmac; I couldn't remember where to go and no one else was about, but the taciturn Major with the jeep didn't budge, just ordered another drink for both of us, without taking his dreadful eyes from my face; it was like a situation in Dostoevsky. He had me trapped, he knew it and it seemed to give him pleasure. We drank all night in silence until the plane left at dawn.

Sitting on the canvas strap along the sides (we were the only passengers) it got colder and colder. The old Dakota bucketed and shuddered, the lashed crates of mortars and ammunition slipped and strained at their ropes. If one broke loose we'd be squashed and the overloaded plane would crash from change of balance; the pilot had said so before we took off. I'd sat up drinking for three consecutive nights now and was sick nearly all the time. The Major sat opposite me, staring, still silent, following me with his eyes when I stumbled to the bucket, and back again. At last he seemed to come to a decision and shoved his face across at me: 'Christ! this is what they make 'em of nowadays!' as though that was what he'd been trying to remember to say all night. After that he didn't look at me any more and went to sleep; I got up and was sick again.

We landed on an American airfield; the Major disappeared like an hallucination, and the plane taxied away. There were no airport buildings, it was a temporary landing-strip, there was nowhere to go and no one to ask. I tried once or twice to find out from a passing American mechanic where we were, but he didn't have time to stop.

After about two hours of this, just standing among the revving Sabre jets while the Yanks played out some desperate war movie (there'd been no fighting for ages, the whole thing was a charade), wondering how long it took to die of cold – and three days without food or sleep – I saw the familiar green of a British lorry. The driver said he dropped by every day in case there was anyone stranded. He thought the Yanks likely to let him starve to death before they noticed and I wondered if he wasn't right. He offered to take me in the direction of our fellow-countrymen. There, after a long day's tracking on foot through the bombed-out ruins of a small mud-town, I came upon a partially demolished wooden school with the name of my unit scrawled on it in chalk. No one was at home, the untidy canvas beds on each side of the schoolroom looked slept-in, but there was a pile of straw in a corner and I was unconscious before I reached the floor.

.

Poked awake by a stick: 'Good God! I thought you were a bundle of washing!' I was given a meal and a bed – rather frigidly, I suppose it wasn't an impressive arrival – and introduced to the journalists.

They were a depressed lot, nothing had happened for ages and their editors found this impossible to believe. They were terrified a story would break and their Fleet Street competitor would get it (that is to say, Pete in the next bed). Their professional frame of mind was that of a child's who is afraid he's missing something; if one of them pulled out his type-writer (the case professionally battered, pasted with the labels of esoteric hotels, punctured here and there with what might be mistaken, by a very small boy, for bullet-holes), or as soon as one of them began to write anything, the others pointed like gun-dogs and sauntered casually behind him, trying to crib. The writer covered up with his elbow, like the school swot.

The telephone system was rudimentary, a green box you had to wind which reached, if lucky, an exchange a good way south, in Seoul, which then transferred the dictated message to Tokyo. You had to keep talking even if there was no one at the other end, otherwise you were cut off. The chant of 'Working-working-working-working' sometimes continued for an hour and when he got through he'd begin his pathetic despatch. 'Today two lucky Geordies from the Royal Northumberland Fusiliers will find they've been chosen to fly home to be guests of honour at the F.A. Cup Final between their home-team Newcastle United and . . . workingworkingworkingOperator – wherethehellareyou OhpleaseOperatorOh CHRIST!' I saw more than one toughguy Hemingway-esque Foreign Correspondent collapse on his bed, his back shaken with manly sobs. His paper wouldn't have a story for that day and his editor would want to know why. Even if he'd got it he probably wouldn't have printed it. I decided I didn't want to be a journalist.

Apart from helping to run this mobile hotel for War Correspondents (they had WC embroidered in gold on their caps – or did I dream that?) I had to go out and collect stories myself in my capacity of War Office Observer. These had to rely on the warm human angle: 'Trooper Higgins of 18, The Lindens, Crouch-on-Sea, smiled as he gave the finishing touch of polish to his already gleaming tank. "Things aren't so bad here. We had beer last month and a couple of weeks ago the lads tried to get up a game of Soccer on the lorry park." ' I wasn't very good at it. I suppose the pieces found their way eventually to local papers, and gave pleasure to worried relatives; I hope so. But I felt ashamed, and was usually too shy to ask the right questions. These were soldiers; I wore a brown uniform too, but what was I?

The job had great advantages, however. I was out all day with a driver and a jeep of my own. I could visit my friends in the battalions, and make my face familiar to the Ulster Rifles. And driving about that inhumanly stark, clay-brown countryside was a strange experience. Ravaged by a sequence of advancing and retreating armies, it was nearly deserted. It was also, at least where we were, nearly without vegetation; a series of deep-sunk serpentine rivers; range after range of symmetrical bare hills like squat brown triangles, and occasionally a deserted village built neatly out of mud. Sometimes you'd see white-robed figures picking hopelessly among ruins, or dead and neglected in a paddy-field, but mostly the local population kept out of sight, waiting for this terrible thing to pass. Except for the hordes of orphaned children; they besieged you everywhere pleading for jobs, five-year-olds clad in huge American army uniforms tossed them by some kindly soldier, their sleeves trailing the ground as they ran after you, their American fatigue caps kept up by their tiny ears. Things were not quite so bad for them now the fearful winter was nearly over and a thin sun was beginning to make that strange landscape even more the colour of the moon. My friends in the line sometimes showed me their frost-blackened fingers, relics of that winter. I had arrived at a lucky time.

I hopefully called on the Ulster Rifles yet again. I was invited up to the Command Post overlooking the valley below their position. Down there was a Company trying to winkle out a sniping machine-gun post. The Company Commander described his plans on the radio and then gave a running commentary on the action as it happened. His voice was clear in the early spring sunshine as we sat comfortably on the hill-top watching the platoons deploy beneath us like toy soldiers in a toy war. The machine-gun post stopped rattling. Presumably the men inside that puff of smoke were dead. One of ours was wounded. The Colonel called up a helicopter on another radio; within moments it was there, settling delicately into the valley like a dragonfly, and the wounded man was on his way to hospital. All highly satisfactory; time to fold up the camp-stools, time for lunch. The Colonel said: 'Do you still want to join us? What about it, John?' The man called John laughed: 'Oh, all right! He can be second-in-command of the Battle Patrol. He can't do much harm there.' 'We'll look after him, sir,' said a fatherly-looking Sergeant. 'Nonsense – make him walk in front! Come to lunch, Patrick.' So we climbed down the hill together. I'd joined the battalion.

I went back to collect my things. One of the journalists watched me packing:

'How old are you?'

'Twenty.'

'For God's sake you've hardly *started* yet! What d'you want to go and put your head in a noose for?'

I didn't know. I only knew I wanted to see what it was like.

Immediately I joined the battalion, for the first time since I came into the Army, for the first time in my life, in those absurd conditions, I felt myself at home.

We moved into the line. And then further forward until I think we were the apex of the whole position across Korea. Every day the Battle Patrol pushed further into the hills looking for the enemy. They were believed to be preparing for an attack. Sometimes we ventured five or six miles from our own lines, with no result.

At Brigade they were puzzled about the invisibility of the enemy. A dotty plan was considered of dropping two men by parachute far behind the enemy lines, disguised as Koreans, with radios. I volunteered; it seems I couldn't get deep enough in. They wouldn't have had me for the job anyway, I imagine, but the plan was abandoned because the enemy appeared, and our patrol was the first to discover them. This happened within ten or fifteen yards of the 38th Parallel, the point of dispute the war was all about; I remembered seeing a post marking it the day before; on Shakespeare's birthday, St George's Day 1951; thirteen years ago. Afterwards I wrote an account of it as faithful as I could make it.

I hope the reader will forgive the sudden change in style

(the racing changes through the gear-box from first to third person, the 'Irishry' perhaps) but I give the story now as I wrote it then, because it is true to how I felt at the time, the disconnectedness; true to the fix that young man was in – like many other young men probably. But the rest of this book is the story of a rescue; and you can only measure the size of a rescue if you know how badly it is needed. I called the story *Boy with Gun*.

AFTER General Absolution he leant over the edge of his slit-trench and listened to the grass growing. The yellow crack of the cliffs forgot to guard the fish-coloured river below, lost between their wide and ancient heights. White dots put out white dots. The cave people, the refugees, trusting tentatively the sun, spread their meagre washing on rocks. He looked along his sights. He could shoot the lot of them even at that immense distance. The bullets would fall plumb-straight and pierce and puncture. Pop goes the weasel. He felt the vibration of the gun, the scatter of the ejected cartridge-cases, smelt the fumes; down below he saw the scurry back to shelter, the few white blobs that remained, beautifully still. A man (twenty years old) with a gun, on a hill. The final simplification. Self-supporting, self-sufficient, content as a *clochard* in his skin of filthy clothes, not even his boots once off in three whole youth-hostelling, gun-toting Robinson Crusoe weeks. He eyed the white homunculi below, Bren-benevolent, their green-coated guardian sitting on the Spring.

'Boys,' Father Ryan had said, puffing after his steep (and courageous) climb, 'some of ye'll not see another day. So if you will all make a good Act of Contrition I'll give you

General Absolution.' He then pronounced the formula and made the sign of the cross over the group of kneeling Irishmen. Some went up for communion, the young regular subalterns among them, giving an example to the men. He didn't. A man with a gun on a hill. His filthy ankles itched comfortably under his gaiters. Anyway, he was absolved, and leaving the Mass tent he climbed back up to his platoon position.

The sun was getting warmer. Spring had really come. He stepped over his slit-trench, found a rock on the forward slope and went to sleep. When the sun moved round the hill the cold woke him up and he sneaked back. Asleep for three hours in No-Man's Land. He wasn't even a good soldier. 'Please God make me a human being.' A man with a gun on a hill.

Sergeant had scrounged from the bombed valley an eiderdown, of all things. On top of the straw it made a luxurious mattress in their sleeping-trench. After standdown, propped on an elbow in their tiny space every night, the Sergeant made mugs of chocolate, meticulous as a nanny; his fuel tablets in one hollow in the trench wall, his chocolate tablets in another, the tiny flame from the burner shielded by his large hands lest the enemy see any glow. Thus he made himself and his bed-companion comfortable. A brave man, the best Sergeant in the battalion; given the most difficult job with this platoon, which was a special service one, his nerves were very tired. He awoke at every rustle, every crack. He could distinguish at night between the different sounds of Very lights; the Chinese ones made a different pop. The first time they had been attacked the Officer had been too deep asleep to disentangle his weapons in the dark. Without reproach the Sergeant had thrust a last-war-looted Luger pistol into his hand. They crawled out, each taking charge of half the platoon on the hill-top. Then he discovered he couldn't cock it. 'Sergeant,' he was forced to whisper across the black, 'how does this thing work?' The Sergeant wriggled across and showed him, again in silence. Thus they got on well together, but non-feudally. The only condition was that the Officer would not come his fortuitous rank over the Sergeant but would, under advice, play his more theatrical role. They understood each other perfectly, neither having the slightest doubt who was the better man. Meanwhile the lovingly prepared chocolate and the knowledge that however deeply he slept the Sergeant would sleep only fitfully, alert, having more to lose than twenty years of scarcely begun life.

Today the Sergeant went on leave. Hm! Does he smell something up? Know he'd pick his leave date carefully, weighing the chances, soldier in that as in all. So tonight all alone on scrounged eiderdown; kind of duck, eider; funny to think of it in one of those valley mud huts – family heirloom probably. Turn on side. Spiked by sten-gun lying in Sergeant's empty place. Made to penetrate the sweet and milky flesh with intent. Neat little holes pocked in taut ten-gallon drums. What else can you do little Sten? Nothing. Nothing! A maniac's toy. Easier to let life out than to let life in. We're trained to penetrate each other to death. Frustrations, Father Ryan, make good soldiers. Free love to end war! (The queues of *mutilés de guerre*, 'Buddy, can you spare a dame?') Women worst, surprisingly. White feathers. 'We don't want to lose you but we think you ought to go'. . . . Wup! Horizontal white face through tent flap. Wanted at H.Q. Here it comes! How long asleep? What time?

Strained faces in the valley. We are to take a patrol into enemy territory, report by wireless on their movements, their number and then return. How very *nice* they're being. Don't they expect us to come back?

The Bren Carriers move off in the white moonlight, their

tracks the only disturbance in the perfect tranquillity of the night. The men are silent, licking their lips; shiver, smelling trouble. And there is indeed a smell of danger; it is too quiet. Odd pops of rockets go up well to their front, funny-coloured, strange. Wish Daddy Sergeant was here. No. He's better off wherever he is.

The deep-sunken river is metallic with moonlight when their cavalcade reaches it, the sand on its white shores silver unturned for millions of years; it seems an outrage to spray it about. And the cave people? Were they gone smelling trouble like the animals they had been forced to become – gone with their white washing to other holes to hide to live again another day? Or were they lying awake in the dark holding each other as the helmeted death-seekers ground whitefaced by, with only cold weapons to hold? They were reported to be a cruel race, during the war (which war? the one before this after the great before the next) used by the Japanese as prison guards. Now it was hard not to see them as guardians, life treasurers, noble fugitives from death – a positive flight.

On the enemy side of the ford approaching a large open space, a gap in the cliffs, they slow down, halt. The senior officer confers with the junior in the offhand shorthand that passes for communication between them.

'Looks a bit fishy.'

'Yes.'

'Better push on a bit, though.'

'Right.'

He screwed his eyes up so tight he saw stars, private semi-voluntary comment on fatuousness. Slowly they move off again, pressing into the tautening membrane of the night. Grind, whirr, whine go the tracks, the engines, a defined envelope of noise in the white moon-silence.

Penetration! The membrane snaps. Flames, rockets, yells,

a thousand Cup Final rattles, Guy Fawkes, one of the carriers in front goes up, whoosh! Christ! Fifty of us have run into a bloody army! Weapons, helmets, wireless sets, all go flying in the mad scramble to get out, back into the womb of the dark away from the red bee-swarms of the tracers.

'Come back,' he shouted. Not quite sure why, except that he didn't particularly fancy being left sitting there alone. Anyway it annoyed his schoolboy sense of order to see them running off into nowhere. Run home by all means, I'll come with you except the river's in the way, but not into the meaningless no-direction dark.

'Stop!'

Some do, uncertainly. A few run on, never to be seen again, ever. He dismounts gingerly from his lonely chariot.

'Lie down, face your front and return the fire.'

Good notion that, keep us occupied for a bit. Irregular spiritless bangs begin around him.

'Get that Bren gun going.'

'There's something wrong with it, Sorr.'

'Mend it.'

Splendid stuff this. And will the First Cavalry, just in the nick, pennants a-flutter come riding riding. . . . No. He wished he wasn't there.

'I can find nothing wrong with this Bren, Sorr, known to God or to man.'

Oh, the Irish, the irresistible cadence, unresisted. Probably too scared to put the thing together properly; time, none the less, for a phrase.

Stage-lit by the moon and the blazing carrier, the other carrier drivers, crouched invisible and blind behind their raised visors of armour, begin to yaw and swerve through the bullets on their way back home. Thinking, presumably, they can be of little use here. One goes over a prone soldier's pelvis.

His scream is a white wall of cold fire; the bullets falter and fall against it.

Morphia. Have little needled ampoules in trousers. Officers only for the control of. Might give Other Ranks other dreams. Stick it in his arm. Can't. 'You do it, Medical Orderly.' That delay an eternity of agony for the dying man. You coward. Couldn't stick a needle in a man's arm. No, couldn't. All right, coward. What to do with him? He can't be carried, must be left, alive, dying of pain.

He only joined us yesterday.

'They've got behind us, sir.'

Irregular shots from the dark back of them. Have an idea it's other officer comrade and remaining rest. Better go look. No point in crawling, take too long, better walk. Up! There! Look they love me they're emitting death rays, love rays. My public! The stinging lines of tracers, slow at first, accelerating and swish! past him. And why are you here anyway strolling through red swinging stars? Everyone did all they could to discourage you, dissuade you. God the Grocer showed me the shop. The ring-a-ling till (with assiduous application chastity and a bright morning face you too may be manager). They even got the ladder out and showed me the contents of the topmost jar, sweets for the sweet. No good. Didn't tickle my palate. But isn't there anyone you're sorry to leave? Mother? No. Father? No. Girl friend? No. (Who the hell else is there?) Brother? No. (He asked me once and I said: No.) Oh, Fathers Ryan Father Ryans, is this where your interpretations of life-love teachings have led me? Or is it in the bone of all of us? For at least I'm not alone, there seem to be plenty of us death-wishers about tonight. Smiling self-consciously he crossed the bullet-sighing dark.

'Take care of yourself, sir.'

Who was that? Hoarse concern. Love. Well, any leader

was better than none; mutual need. Curious that warmed so much. Wonder who it was? Figures loom out of the black. Livingstone I presume? . . . I'm a dead duck if not. . . .

'Brian?'

'Ah!'

Sheepish at having retreated further than his junior, Brian began to give terse textbook orders, obviously at sea, as well he might be.

'Get your men on their feet. We'll retire to a defensive position in that clump of trees over there.'

'But Brian, don't you think that . . .'

'Come on. Hurry!'

'Right.'

Defensive position my Aunt Fanny! Where does he think he is, Salisbury Plain? What's left of fifty of us taking on the whole bloody Chinese army. What we should be doing is getting out of here fast. On either side men drop as they move across the open field to the trees. There all is confusion. It seems for a moment as if there are enemy soldiers there too, only the curses sound reassuring.

'Sir, Leary's got hurt on the way across. Can I go and get him, sir?'

'No.'

'But he's my mukker, sir!'

Blank consternation. Greater love than this. . . . Another face, contorted, is thrust into his –

'Sir, there's one of 'em moving about just down there. Shall I kill him, sir? shall I kill him? I'll throw this at him.' Brandishing a grenade, hopping up and down. You'd have his head in your knapsack too, wouldn't you, you blood-crazy little bastard. Takes people different ways apparently.

'Shall I kill-kill-kill um, sir?'

'No.'

From the shadows in front of them the figure got up, seemed to fall down. If one of theirs surely wounded. Just possibly one of ours, Leary too hurt to cry out.

'No.' Here's Brian.

'I'll stay here with Corporal, three others and non-walking wounded. You take the rest back across the river. We'll give you covering fire and join you when you're across.'

Of all the fatuous plans! He's condemning himself and the others to death. Chances are we won't get through anyway and if he stays he certainly won't. Try to explain. All together. Can't leave you.

'That's an order.'

'Right.'

Move into chaste silver field, brilliant after the infested dark of the trees, holding out arms at an angle as though to draw the frightened men with him.

'Arrow head formation. Follow me.'

Close on me, Scouts! No one moves. Can hardly blame them. Neither would I. Better the evils that we know. They want to see what is going to happen to me. What *is* going to happen to me? The river looks a long way away.

Brrp.

Find face deep in earth. Instinctive fall. Raise head a little. Brrp. It's that lurching fellow the dancing maniac wanted to do in. Suicide pilot out to get the officer. Gingerly raise Sten, can just get him in sights – only about twenty yards away. Suddenly the empty field surrounding our privacy seems enormous. We are alone, face to face, belly-flat. Can't pull trigger. Can't. Don't like the sound of the silence that would follow. What a soldier! Brrp. That's it. It's a burp gun, fast firing from a large magazine makes a noise like a belch. He's firing in little bursts, taking his time, determined to get me, knows he's had it anyway. Much good may it do him. What about your wife and kids back on the collective farm? Collective wife and kids maybe. Not worth dying for, not worth living for. Hail brother trying to kiss me by proxy. Sorry I don't seem able to kiss you back. This thing is bigger than both of us.

Brrp.

He's getting the angle now. That burst was about two inches in front of my cap badge. Wonder if it shines in the moonlight. You've come a long way and tried very hard to reach this moment. And they've really laid it on for you. It would be quite impossible to be nearer death, to be more physically comfortable and to have more time to think about it.

Brrp.

Damn! Some of the earth spurted into my ear. Tickles. Better not move to scratch, only makes bigger target. Think. I'm sure all our listeners would like to know what were your impressions under fire. Fear? No. Odd, even horrible, but no. See if I can feel some. Next burst will probably go through the top of my head. Won't know any more. General Absolution. Or a shoulder. Painful but will still be able to walk. One along my spine would paralyse me. Left here conscious to die like that other chap. Fear? Yes, maybe, but unlikely shot that. Little soft slug bouncing along my vertebrae like a stick along railings. What the hell kind of world am I in is in me that I can think of such things without outrage? If I'm not afraid at least I should be angry. But I'm not. No.

Brrp.

He's wandered a bit to the right that time. He's a bloody bad shot. General Absolution. . . . Good God!

According to the rubric of the Catholic One Holy and Apostolic the faith of my fathers I've got a fully franked visa to the Beatific Vision impossible even for me to mislay. There isn't enough time. But to give up the God-given Ghost with so little enthusiasm either way? Perhaps this is the Sin

Against The Holy Ghost? (Please Father what *is* the Sin Against The Holy Ghost? Hush, my child. Hm. Must be something pretty horrible. Always knew babies didn't grow on gooseberry bushes.)

Fuck!

Through my shoulder. Burrowing softly through the soft flesh out under my arm spent into the earth. Penetration. Onan cast his seed upon the ground. Another foreskin bites the dust. Curious how feeble sad and disappointed it felt as it left me. . . .

For God's sake! I'm playing woman to some Chink's phallic belch gun.

'Can't somebody do something about this bugger?' A cry to galvanise the boys, to make me human again. They've been witnesses of a blood sacrifice for long enough. Bang! right in my ear. Is this the end? No, one of them's come out and let off his rifle by my head. Oh, what a silence follows! Up and back to cover.

He's lying very still out there, crumpled and curiously flat now, like a tyre punctured, as though the earth were already greedily sucking him down. I feel nothing for him at all, no hate, no pity, just nothing.

Morphia from the other officer among trees. He doesn't hesitate with the needle and still insists on original plan.

Out into the moonlight again, the men slowly following this time, thinking perhaps that if anyone could emerge alive from that his luck must be in. The enemy are everywhere and very close indeed; some of them stand up to get a better look, dun-coloured, queer-shaped in their padded uniforms, mysterious. Once again no point in crawling. They could kill the lot of us in about thirty seconds flat vertical or sideways and it's quicker *debout*. Glad no one feels like talking. The enemy seem hypnotised, like a crowd watching a trapeze-act beginning to wobble. It seems that one word, one stumble even would break the spell and the weird watching figures would remember themselves, remember to shoot. If only Brian has the instinct *not* to give us his pea-shooter covering fire. But he too seems hypnotised. This silence is fantastic. . . . I can hear the jags in the breath of the man five men away from me, the one with the smashed arm. It's against all the rules, we're walking through the watching enemy . . . it's crazy! They've let us get as far as the sand of the river! Better quicken things up a bit. Single file. Six-hundred yards, five-hundred, four-hundred, the ford is coming into sight now. They're still popping up and down to look at us. Can't believe their eyes, I suppose. Perhaps they think we couldn't behave so foolishly unless we had a plan – were acting as decoys perhaps? It only needs one trigger-happy sod to set them all off. And now, the ford! Why doesn't Brian join us, now we've got this far? He's no use where he is and they're bound to wake up in a minute. Officer-like, captain on sinking bridge, let men file across first, holding pistol vaguely towards enemy. Forgot to load it suddenly remember. One man stays with me.

'Thin red line, eh?'

Gets the contemptuous silence it deserves. Morphia taking effect? Nice of him to stay though.

Across! Now wait for Brian.

There is a kind of knob, an atoll in the small sea of sand that is the beginnings of the narrow defile between the cliffs and the sharp hills behind them that is their way home. Dispose the men about it, prone, covering the ford, waiting for Brian. Silence. Still this twanging tingling silence. Oh, Brian and your five come on come on. If he doesn't come do I go and get him?

For the first time he allowed himself to acknowledge the sluggishly moving maggot in his brain: his inability to think of the terribly maimed on the other side of the river, and his relief that he wasn't with them. He had thirty-odd men and himself to get home, a task he could face; leading a retreat to safety seemed to him, of all warlike activities, the most worth while. But there were the maimed and dying on the other side of the river. There always are.

Sir, my mukker's out there. Can I get him? The urgency and purity of love; that was revealed.

Can I kill'um k-k-kill'um? Two faces. He could look in neither. Instead he stared across the river into the dark hostility opposite, pent, ready to explode.

Then they heard what they had been dreading. The faint pathetic sputtering of Brian's few weapons, the cries and banshee yells of a small enemy attack going in. And then, again, silence. His mind shied from thinking of what had happened. Suddenly, as though it had digested a minor snack, the full-scale flaming breath of the dragon was turned scorchingly on them. The whole river bank opposite their tiny position seemed to burst into noise and fire. No hope for Brian this way now.

'Retreat.'

He walked among the stunned soldiers, most of them with their faces pressed deep into the stony ground, waiting for the end, for deliverance. God in a modern morality play he tapped the blind ones on the back with his toy pistol and bade them rise and walk.

'Retreat. Form up on the road below. And don't run.'

Somehow it seemed that if one of them should run it would be the end, they should all be killed. Some of the men couldn't hear him, deafened by the noise, so he had to walk to each, waiting, when they lifted their heads to look at him, for consciousness to return to their wide, blank eyes. He found their lack of heroism warming.

Soon they were all up and away and he prepared to join them. Stopping, he suddenly thought that perhaps one in the dark and the noise might not have heard, might still be lying there alone with his eyes shut. Better go back and check. He seized upon it as a tiny conscience-saver. They, the living, had left and were now finally abandoning the nearly dead, and he had been forced to look at his own relief. So he walked again through the pretty bright bullet-birds, meticulously traversing the little plateau back and forth, as though looking for a lost golf ball, and surrendered himself to a healing flow of self-approval; but he knew that none of those thousands of burning sparks would pierce him a second time. The patient had been found insufficiently alive for the sweet anaesthetic. This was only a pause before he turned back to where his real fear lay, the dead dragging weight of his fear of life. He was not to be let off so lightly.

Having satisfied himself there was no one remaining, he climbed down to the road where the men were waiting in numbed silence. They led off while he followed behind. It was still a beautiful night and the narrow road was a white thread through the dark triangular pattern of the hills. As they walked they became aware that these hills, near enough almost to touch, were alive with figures, advancing upon their lines. An enormous attack was mounting. The straw-covered feet of the enemy soldiers pitter-pattered up the angle of an isosceles hill – pause – pitter-patter down; a nightmare see-saw motion of unimaginable marathon toughness; looking neither right nor left, scarcely breaking their stride to hop over the bodies of those who had fallen, while he and his little band walked, unmolested, pursuing their civilian way along the road, leaving the hills to the soldiers. They would get through, he knew they would; and they did.

At the first tent of their advance lines that was near the road they stopped and he went in to use the field telephone; he had to report back to the battalion. That, after all, was the purpose of the exercise. He could hear Brian putting it like that. (Brian! How could he explain? He was alive and where was Brian?)

The young doctor was already quietly busy with the first casualties. The firing was now very close. He was awkward in his handling of the phone.

'Here! You all right?'

'Yes.'

'Let me see.'

Cuts away material of camouflage smock. Funny. Tidy little hole. Neat sweet lips. . . .

'You've had morphia.'

Statement not question. Must be sounding odd. Giggling perhaps?

'You're staying here.'

Ah well, job done I suppose. Would much rather get back to the battalion, however. Firing *very* close – wouldn't like to be trapped in this tent, felt much safer in the open dark. The old image of the pop of bullets into a taut surface, aural, visual, tactual, made him look apprehensively at the tent roof. Then at the entrance flap. Perhaps soon entry of yapping foreign-featured strange-clothed semi-men, fearsome because unknown, primitively frightening, numinous. He got up quickly.

'Where are you going?'

'Just for a breath of air.'

His men were slowly filing back to the battalion, their steps lighter than for many hours; having got thus far, within smell of their comrades, had no further use for him.

'Goodbye.'

Opposite the tent a Colonel was crying at the crossroads into a broken telephone. Of the old school, he had known most of his men personally, their villages, their backgrounds. Suddenly, within minutes, he had none left.

Inside, the doctor continued about his business, while the

firing seemed to come to the very door of the tent; he would almost certainly be taken prisoner, but he seemed quite unconcerned with his own safety. Perhaps he at least was truly brave.

At last an ambulance arrived, as far as his nerves were concerned not a moment too soon. It was already full. He settled himself into the only vacant corner with a sigh – forced to hold his head at a certain angle to avoid the drip of blood from the soldier on the cot above. After a while the dripping stopped and he could sit more comfortably, the soldier having died.

THE SIGHTS and smells of that time in Korea (the sounds I could have done without but even they gave pleasure to some: 'Nothing like a good bang' they'd say, with shining faces); the smell of the meagre brushwood we somehow gathered on our hillsides for fires (it reminded me of cherry, I don't know why, I've never been able to trace it) and the smell of the American tinned rations we put unopened into the water of the billycans until the scum on it (we'd used it to wash in) heaved and bubbled – these lingered on your body and everyone else's, neither pleasant nor unpleasant, but unlike any other. The faces of those who'd been out all winter were wind- and frost-burnt, like a yellow tan, and plus the grey dust from the springtime roads which seemed to settle in your pores this gave them a greeny tinge, but healthy and tough; and with the wind and the oil and the dust their hats had become strangely coloured too, shaped dashingly to their heads, and their overalls had the same patina, fitting them snugly like skins. They'd achieved an archaic, all-in-one-piece look; you thought: they've become warriors.

The noise and dust of the trucks, open jeeps skidding to a halt like broncos, greetings waved from hillsides, files of men singing quietly as they sloped along at dusk, flickering lights at night in the pup-tents, whisky drunk out of tins and the fresh-air-burnt faces crowded together round the one candle. Above all the sense of experience shared and a kind of equality, even in the rigid British army, most of all that. There wasn't any room left for the old class fears, at least for a while. In spite of the schoolboy rubbish, comradeship existed, one of the beautiful things.

But all this belongs to another story. Except the last. Once you've had a glimpse of that, whatever the circumstances, and felt how it made your bones lie easy, the absence of it worries you, you've a sense of deprivation.

•

The ambulance dropped us off at a commandeered school somewhere further south; an American orderly shaved the hair in my arm-pit with a blunt razor-blade held between finger and thumb, and I climbed on to a kitchen table for the operation. I'd had to wait a long time, the place was crowded out, the corridors jammed with stretchers; Americans, Turks, Belgians, Chinese, Koreans, some of them lying very still, their faces waxy. I guessed the attack had been as big as it had seemed, we were only the beginning.

In fact the assault (they were forming-up when we ran into them) was a huge one; several hundred thousand men were involved. As we were walking along the road that night the figures on either side were running towards the Gloucesters, whom they overran; I think there were only thirty-odd survivors out of six or seven hundred, and their Colonel won the V.C. The other regiment of our brigade, the Northumberland Fusiliers, didn't do much better, lost a lot of men, including two of my friends from the cabin. My own battalion had been put in reserve the day before, handing over our forward hill to the Belgians – bearded, wild-looking men, and so were a little back from the line. Even so we lost a great many too, and only managed to get out because the 8th Hussars allowed us to jump on their tanks. Next day (the day I lay in the schoolroom) we brought our artillery down on the enemy advance – they didn't have any them-selves – but it made no difference. They never wavered al-though bunches died as each salvo landed. There'd been much talk of 'Chinese hordes' – I once heard an Irish soldier ask an American: 'How many companies is it to a Horde?' – but faced with such numbers, and such soldiers, there was nothing to do but run. I never discovered what happened to the Belgians stuck out on our old hill where I'd put all the trip flares, an island in an advancing sea. I'd be surprised if many of them survived.

Brian and his handful of men swam the river, dragging the wounded with them. He'd meant me to do the same, not cross by the ford, which seemed too far away. This had never occurred to me and my unmilitary-mindedness saved our lives. The enemy avoided the road, kept to the hills, and so Brian ran smack into them, and they were taken prisoner. They were about to be shot by an officer with a pistol when something distracted his attention (perhaps he didn't relish the task) and he ran off. Brian covered the wounded with bracken and decided to try to get through on his own. As he moved away one of our own mortar bombs landed on them. He wandered about for a couple of days and eventually reached the battalion, not making much sense, carrying two empty cases of mortar-bombs from which he refused to be parted. It is cruel to die, and cruel to survive.

All this I learned later – that the battle came to be known as the Battle of the Imjin River – and that it drove back the United Nations army hundreds of miles. Well, the first shots of that battle were fired at us. As for the Gloucesters, whose weapons I'd heard all round the tent I'd telephoned from (it was the Gloucesters' doctor whose coolness I'd so much admired), their effort that night was described by the American Admiral Van Fleet as 'the greatest example of unit bravery in modern times.'

But now, after a spell in an American hospital in the southern tip of Korea, I was sitting on an airstrip in American pyjamas, clutching my sponge-bag with my empty revolver in it, mildly gangrenous, waiting for the plane to take us to base hospital. That revolver was a nuisance; but like Brian and his cases of mortar-bombs I wouldn't hand it over. I remembered something about throwing away your weapons in the face of the enemy. I felt I might be called to account for it: 'And where, Kavanagh, is your revolver? You *left* with one, I believe?' Various hospital officials tried to take it away from me; it was a ridiculous thing to have as your only piece of luggage – especially in pyjamas – but I clung on to it. Partly because it helped me with my guilt about Brian and his few. Had I done right to leave them? What else could I have done? It went round and round in my mind, but at least I had my revolver. I had 'withdrawn', I hadn't run away. Nevertheless, my nerve hadn't been tested and I'd learned nothing. It was all over before I'd begun.

There was another puzzle, sitting all day on that airstrip: the apparent eagerness for death I'd been showing all these months. And worse: the way, when faced with it, I'd cared so little. This was startling. I hadn't the equipment to think it out.

And was it true? At some stage of my War Office Observer career I'd decided, in one of those flashes of certainty that come sometimes, that I wanted to go to Oxford if I ever got out of this. It might do something for my terrible ignorance. So I wrote to the Warden of Merton because one of the lay-masters at school had been to that college. I had a suspicion that all was not well at home, that my father was in serious financial difficulties, but how to pay could be worked out later, the first thing was to get a place, and writing to ask for one seemed the simplest way.

So perhaps, if I was making plans, I didn't want to die after all? But why the terrible indifference? It seemed I didn't care for myself very much, or for anybody else. So my mind revolved during those days of the slow evacuation south. For distraction I tried to speak to the Americans I was surrounded with, but had no success; they never seemed to understand what I said, their eyes when they looked at you were coated with wax; their ears too I presumed. They pretended their wounds were worse than they were – this I found reasonable, they wanted to get home and good luck to them – but why then did they also boast to each other about how brave they'd been? Their obvious reluctance to be soldiers seemed to me hopeful for the future; if people don't like fighting then maybe there won't be wars. But why were they so beastly to each other? The Polacks bullied the Swedes, the Swedes bullied the Eyties and even the Negroes bullied whoever they dared. When a huge Negro called over the refugee Korean orderly who was sweeping out the ward, took his dustpan from him and emptied the contents over the floor saying: 'Now sweep it again, Gook!' I reckoned he had plenty of scores to pay off. But I didn't expect the whole ward to laugh, forty Americans of different ages, races, classes, all to laugh, and not one word of even gentle protest.

Waiting on the airstrip, to stop myself thinking I tried again to engage some American in conversation. I was wearing no badges of rank (difficult in pyjamas) so it couldn't have been the 'bloody officer' thing I'd heard them go on about (it didn't seem possible their officers could be as lazy and cowardly as they all agreed they were) but they still walked past, or called out over my shoulder as though I wasn't there, so I engaged in derisive dumbshow with a cheerful Turk who seemed to agree with me, and after a few hours the plane came in to land.

I was convinced I had been meant to die. God had slipped up somehow, or changed his mind.

As the plane circled I saw its tail dip dangerously and I suddenly saw what was going to happen. We would crash on the way to Japan and I'd die that way; the account would be made straight. As we filed on to it I reckoned those who'd die first, and least painfully, would be the ones nearest the front; so I settled myself behind the pilot and went to sleep. We landed without mishap.

.

A slow journey, through more hospitals (one of them American, of astonishing efficiency and kindliness . . .) back at last to the one in Kure, the place I'd left only a couple of months before. I arrived late at night and was shown to a darkened ward which I could see, even in the gloom, contained a number of old friends. I was glad to be back.

In the morning I was woken by the sheet being lifted from my face, and I stared up at the Staff Sister who had been with the Matron when they'd switched on the light in the Sisters' Mess and found me there with a nurse, on Christmas Eve. She was smiling lovingly down at her new patient; Oh! she said, at the sight of me, and quickly dropped the sheet.

The wound healed fast, apparently it was a sort of fluke: the bullet itself, going in at the top of my shoulder and coming out under my arm, missing bone, artery and nerve, an anatomical miracle; and the unknown (American) hands that had cleaned it out on the kitchen table were also a wonder, so dangerous was what they'd done, so well had they done it. I was oppressed by a slightly crazy feeling of unreality. My wound was called a G.S.W. (Gun-Shot Wound) safely distanced by the antique phrase and then reduced further by initials, and I was surrounded by people in various degrees of mutilation, some of it horrible, and no one seemed to see how abnormal it was, maiming each other and patching each other up, or digging a hole and scattering earth over anyone past patching. I couldn't see it myself, it kept slipping away from me.

Anyway it was all over for me before I'd really begun. A kind letter came from the Warden of Merton, waiving the entrance examination, giving me a place. This meant that to get there by the beginning of term I'd have a few days lopped off my National Service, would probably have to go back by the next boat. I was to all intents finished with Korea, and the Army. But what was it I'd missed, that I'd been trying to find?

I knew a lot of people in the hospital, and outside it, and so I had visitors and presents and bedside parties, and this served to inflame the already passionate dislike of the Staff Sister. She managed never to speak to me directly, but always through her subordinate nurses, whom she bullied all day. She was obviously a woman with an excess of energy and worked some of it off on me. It was real hatred, something which frightened me very much. Her particular pet, on the other hand, was Chris Nixon, a Major in my battalion. She discovered he was a baronet, and angrily berated the orderly who had made out his bed-card incorrectly; made the new one out herself, writing Major *Sir* Christopher Nixon, D.S.O. *Bart* with loving care. Chris was a wild man, his body a patchwork of wounds from various wars, his chest a nestful of medals, but gentle and funny as well, generous with the bottle of whisky under his pillow. He was the only one who could make her laugh. I think if she'd thought a curtsey proper she'd have dropped one.

I was in no mood to humour her, but I should have known she'd have the last word. When the time came to leave hospital I was given fourteen days' convalescent leave; I saw her whisper to the doctor in charge – he looked at her, shrugged, and she scribbled in the leave book – fourteen days were changed to seven.

·

Mio Jama was a sort of Paradise Island, no one was allowed to die there. If they looked like doing so their families ferried them quickly to the mainland. The streets among the pines were strung with coloured paper lanterns, there were temples everywhere, decorated with flowers; and the sound of gongs. In the water, that burned yellow-green at night in the slow wake of the fishing boats, there were orange-painted *torii*, the two upright poles with cross bars, curved and delicately proportioned, symbol I was told of how the singing birds tempted the Sun out of his cave and made him shine again. The girls wore their spring kimonos and gorgeous parasols; it was Pinkerton Japan all right, and at that time we, the convalescing soldiers, were the only foreigners on the island.

A hard-bitten, gaunt Australian, who seemed to be convalescing not from wounds but from delirium tremens, told me that he knew the island from way back, and on it was the most famous geisha house in Japan, the real thing – if he had a chat with the *mama-san* would I care to join him? I said I would, and a French-Canadian made a third.

On the appointed night we made our way through the green, quiet streets to the outskirts of the village until we came to an exquisite gabled house standing by itself in a grove, surrounded by sweet-smelling blossoming trees. We were welcomed by a distinguished old lady, bowing low. I didn't care much for the bowing, but no time for scruples now. We squatted on the floor in front of a huge Technicolor feast of rapidly congealing seafood, while the old lady removed our shoes. I hadn't any appetite. A paper partition slid quietly back – a hand appeared, curling gracefully from the wrist, then a shining-black, complicated head, stuck with ornamental skewers, then a plump body wrapped in layers of flowered silk, followed by another, prostrating themselves in front of us. Only two: the Aussie and the Canadian quickly established their claims and this was followed by a lengthy pantomime of giggling and archness from the girls, as they coaxed tit-bits into the men's mouths. The party seemed to be going with a swing and the third girl was expected any moment, she was on her way from the mainland. . . . I walked out of the house towards the steep little street under the swinging lanterns.

'P'treek!' The others must have told her my name. I quickened my step – I always seemed to be running away these days but this wasn't how I wanted the first time to be – nothing, anywhere, was as I wanted it.

'P'treek!' and slatted wooden shoes broke into a hobbled run down the stone steps, an infinitely appealing sound. It was cruel to go on so I turned and there was the girl, a grave little face under the candle lantern hanging from a low tree; eyes puzzled, interrogative, not cajoling; infinitely more sympathetic than the other mechanical dolls. She held out her hand so I took it and we went back together.

She soon stopped the kneeling and giggling at my earnest entreaty, it seemed with relief. She was intelligent and gentle and I stayed with her. Strange noises and guffaws came from behind the other partitions and at one point the Australian slid his back and stood in the dark, grotesque in his shirt-tails, hoarsely whispering encouragement.

In the morning the others, after haggling, went off but my girl asked me to come back to where she lived. I liked her and I stayed for a while but I didn't enjoy being separated from the others; we'd been after the same thing, this was no different, a magazine story merely – me with my

Hemingway-wound in bandages, shacked-up with a little geisha.

Perhaps I was being offered something I wasn't ready for. Perhaps I wasn't being offered anything. I spent most of that morning in her tiny scrupulously clean paper house wondering if it would insult her if I gave her money. And they would want to know where I was at the hotel; I was still in the Army. So I left her; it was over. I did offer her money; she took some of it and folded my fingers back over the rest. At the hotel I lay on my bed and thought.

·

Back at the barracks I waited for my boat. There was a new Colonel, an old-maidish one sent out from England to run the depot, which is how battalions get rid of their unwanted officers. He went entirely by the book and was one of those men whom advice, or even information, seems to make angry. One night we were warned of the possible approach of a typhoon. I imagine he looked up 'Typhoons, action at the approach of' in some military manual, because he paraded the whole barracks on the square in the middle of the night; several soldiers suffered concussion from flying tiles and the typhoon never arrived; this was just as well because he made me Typhoon Officer. I was equipped (as per regulations apparently) with one sponge-bag, one blanket, and one revolver (looters, for the shooting of). I reported to the shaggy Australians who were plotting the course of the typhoon over cups of tea, and the revolver particularly amused them: 'Ker-ist! Here comes Horatio!'

My idleness, which I was bad at disguising, obviously worried this Colonel. He thought I was just out from England and never gave me a chance to tell him otherwise; he never allowed anyone to tell him much, I think it muddled him. He walked round the camp alone, looking severe and frightened at the same time; a sad figure. I was still officially convalescing, but I foresaw a spell of stick-leaning coming up so I hurriedly scrounged myself a job as disc-jockey on the Occupation Forces radio. Every afternoon I did the request programme. I found one song I enjoyed very much; it was a tale of love on the high-trapeze, and went:

> How the sun will shine
> When Zeena the Queen-a
> The up-town arena
> Is mine, all mine.

I played it two or three times every afternoon; no one complained – perhaps I made it a hit.

I had friends outside the camp, Australians and Americans. One Australian couple wanted me to settle in Australia after I left the Army. They'd been years in Japan and I asked them when they were going home: 'Us?' they said, startled, 'we've *been* there!'

I was astonishingly and complicatedly seduced by an American woman. I didn't run away this time, I liked her; but I ran all the way home afterwards, as though the air might blow what had happened away. My inability to connect this with love, and all the things I expected of it, seemed to me the same as my inability to connect bullets with death, or death with not being alive. In fact I felt completely disconnected, alien, and what was worse, couldn't imagine not feeling like that. As nearly as possible I tried to be drunk all the time.

My friends in the Mess were older than I was. Under their jolliness, their constant but unboastful drinking, I sensed the same kind of unspecified dismay and anxiety that I was feeling. It was as though they'd reached the same stage in their lives as I had, when the question: What's the point? had to be dealt with – so they drank and were kind to each other. It was possible to be hearty with them, and drown out the big questions because that avoidance was what we had in common. Patrick Sarsfield couldn't understand this, and I couldn't explain.

On my last night they gave me a party; or rather they made me the excuse for doing what we always did, drink too much. Chris Nixon was master of the revels, put ashtrays on the strings of the piano and, cigarette stuck in the corner of his mouth, played music-hall songs, the strings jangling agreeably, honky-tonk, under the ashtrays. The new Colonel, idiotically, tried to stop us, arriving from his bungalow in a dressing-gown; Chris just beamed deafly, thumping fortissimo; short of court-martialling a roomful of senior officers who were doing what they had a perfect right to do anyway, he couldn't pick on me the only junior present, he could do nothing but trail pathetically back to bed. However else I'd failed, I'd reached, I'd become a member of, the battalion.

A couple of years later I met Chris in England; we went out together, he and his wife and a few others. It was ages since I'd seen him – this last night in fact – and the mood was long gone; I felt he was being friendly to someone who no longer existed, perhaps never had, and we went to places I couldn't afford. I liked him very much, but I felt if he knew me better he wouldn't like me at all. He was just the same, but at one point became serious and said to me quietly: 'Look, we're sorry about that show.' He meant the patrol, and was going to say more, hesitated, and then someone interrupted. Perhaps I was about to have what had happened sorted out for me. But the moment passed and I was too shy to ask.

•

The boat journey was the same in reverse; only I had changed. That I'd been put in for a medal gave me a certain kudos with my companions which I enjoyed. I was beginning to learn by what easy counters it was necessary, on one level, to live. No need to make a production number of the truth, even if you knew it, which was unlikely. But how I'd enjoyed the companionship of the battalion, even for so brief a time! And how astonishing some people were under stress, in danger; instinctively willing to give their life for a particular friend; ordinary, unheroic men from the factories of Belfast, with no stake in glory. And the senseless horror of the maiming and killing, which no one could admit fully enough, it was too big to hold in the head. Horror and beauty; a world was taking shape.

I WANDERED about the High Street, Carfax, Cornmarket – magical names – looking for an all-night chemist, wanting a comb. I'd forgotten to bring one and next day gentlemen were requested to call on all sorts of people, to do things with mediaeval Latin names, and after two years in the Army it seemed essential to be combed. It was astonishing to be there at all, with a recognised role, *in statu pupillari* as the college notice-board put it, walking the shoddy-suburban streets with the grey quadrangles waiting peacefully behind them, in one of which I had my allotted cave.

It had turned out a particularly gloomy niche I'd been given, one not normally used, a dark bed-sitter with a small window opening on to the pavement of Merton Street; and my scout was a woman (a big let-down that) who had only one breast as she told me straight away. But it was indeed astonishing I should be there, result of a letter written thousands of miles away, with someone standing over me at the tent-pole despairingly winding the telephone – 'WorkingWorkingWorking! . . .' Unknown to me my father, broke, had cancelled my place, and my rooms had been given to someone else. On his own initiative my brother had written to the college cancelling this letter (and I owe him a lot for that); I'd scrounged a County Scholarship and with a guaranteed minimum for existence I'd confirmed the whole thing with the by now bewildered but always polite college authorities, and they'd found me the last corner they had left. The first undergraduate for thirty years to be given a place without an entrance examination, I'd made it at the last possible moment.

Partly I envied the other undergraduates the air they had of taking for granted they should be there – stepping immediately into college life, joining Societies, having coffee in each other's rooms. I felt immeasurably older than they were, and hollow. Confronted incredulously with Virgil, with Anglo-Saxon grammar, with the to me unreadable *Samson Agonistes* – it was three years since I had done any work of that kind – I found it impossible to take the place seriously. On Guy Fawkes night I went to sleep to the sound of fireworks and dreamt that Chinamen were climbing into my room from Merton Street carrying machine-guns, and I had to warn the porter at the lodge. I woke up in the quadrangle on my way to him.

Patrick Sarsfield had warned me to be careful to choose my friends, not to get lumbered at the outset with some unrewarding fellow who happened to live on the staircase. This seemed the best of advice and I sturdily withstood all overtures. I now think we should allow life to choose our companions for us, our own choice is sure to be too narrow – mine certainly was. I'd no idea what my principle of selection should be and endless unrewarding fellows were sent away unrewarded; I refused to join all societies, even the Oxford University Interdenominational Christian Union which was touted by a gentle Chinese of such patience that I came to regard his presence in my room, quietly holding out a card inviting me to their Tea, as in some way permanent.

Most evenings I spent writing verse. Looking at some of it again it doesn't seem too bad, but as my tutor said more than once: 'Most young men write verse'. (He made it sound like acne, with the implication: If you do, for God's sake don't show me.) Not that I would have, I was rather ashamed of it; the poems in the University magazines seemed so much more accomplished, I felt I had to wait until I got cleverer; and the one time I went to a literary society the rather beady earnestness (and then the cluster round the visiting celebrity, a possible contact for the future) made me want to sing a comic song or shout 'Up the' Spurs'. A conceited reaction, but self-protective as well. The company of some fellow-poets deprived me, temporarily, of the desire ever to write another line.

A university is a terrible place for that, in some ways. If your contemporaries don't put the boot in you're still likely to be snuffed out altogether, unless you're particularly big-headed, by the impossibility of ever being good enough, in terms of what's been done; the same negative humility that afflicts the better dons. I think I must have sensed all this at the time because I showed my poems to no one, avoided the company of other versifiers, and concentrated on the only academically unfiltered experience Oxford had to offer – the marvellous girls. People talk, even Kingsley Amis talks, of unattractive blue-stockings. He must have gone about with his eyes on the ground.

.

One activity I did have to take part in. It was gently hinted that because of my vaguely theatrical connections I was expected to take a part in the College play. As I was very grateful to the College and had already conceived a passion for its buildings and its gardens and its smell, I felt this was fair. I played the offended father in an eighteenth-century translation of *Le Cid*, and undergraduates in other colleges asked me to their parties and offered me parts, and in that way I partially entered the life of the University. But most of the time I spent wooing a Polish goddess up the Iffley Road, or drinking with my ex-boat-companions from Korea. They were hearties – just the people Patrick had told me to avoid – but we enjoyed each other's company, and seemed to have more in common than we had with anyone else.

My tutor, a ruddy, white-haired uncle in smart tweed, obviously looked back on his First World War experience with enthusiasm, and was delighted with the idea of me. 'We took you from the trenches! The trenches!' he used to chortle, and I hadn't the heart to tell him I found this less interesting than he did. In that marvellous room, haven of so many of my hopes, with a huge bay-window looking over the golden Meadows, we even discussed the relative efficacy of various types of machine-gun. He would then ask me to read my essay with an air of apology, as though man to man, between soldiers, these things were a regrettable triviality. And my essay would be extremely dull, barely concealing the boredom I felt with Sir John Davies, or the *Faerie Queene*.

Once I took his between-equals performance at face value and having dutifully read the relevant texts didn't write an essay at all, deciding that a discussion would be more fruitful than a written-out string of commonplaces – I might actually learn something. He leapt from his chair in a pet: 'No essay! No essay!' he cried, snapping his fingers: 'Remember! We took you from the trenches!' . . . as if to say 'Dr. Barnardo's Home and don't you forget it'.

I suppose I should have changed my tutor, as some of his impatient and scholarly American pupils did, but I didn't want to hurt him and anyway I felt sure I was at least partly to blame for the charade we played out between us. What's more, he left me alone, which is what I wanted above all things.

I was bored I think, and frightened; difficult to say of what, of not coming up to scratch I suppose, of finding myself and life some kind of sell. Certainly the latter didn't seem up to much; a struggle, demanding the dreary virtue of staying-power, towards an end that was both doubtful and uninspiring. He makes me so impatient, this remote cousin of more than a decade ago, that I have to be careful. He can't really have been such a sulky lout; he had friends, and enough prestige-type girls paid him attention to keep his vanity in good order. But *did* he have friends? Acquaintances certainly, was even rather popular, enjoying that; and there were two or three to talk with excitedly into the night in the approved University fashion. But he was quite certain there wasn't a soul who felt the way he did, to whom he could explain himself. Words were for passing the time, drink was for the illusion of fellowship and the blurring of distinctions. Where was the simplicity and immediacy he'd seen only a few months before, that had felt like a rebirth; was it only bullets that made this possible? Perhaps this is the beginning of what psychopaths feel, or perhaps it is stupidly commonplace; anyway it's boring; but important for the understanding of what follows, the inertia that had to be overcome.

His emotions were powerful, but turned inwards destructively, and he hid this, just withdrew, remembering to smile as he did so (master of the situation) and then back to his room, back to his pacing round inside himself; raging against imperfections, in himself, in others. He daydreamed fiercely of a perfect love – perfect understanding – he would find it, he must! Meanwhile taking every precaution that it shouldn't find him, he walked around with his head down so as not to see anybody, and kept his eyes blurred so the dream couldn't be interrupted. In this way, not surprisingly, I banged into my tutor, who grasped me and stared while I struggled to bring his face into focus. Sudden, delighted comprehension was shining from it: 'My dear boy! You've just had an *experience*! Tell me! No! Not if you'd rather not . . . later perhaps?' He was quite excited, could hardly wait. It was clear what sort of experience he thought I'd had. Poor old fellow, what was going on inside me wasn't his worry. God knows, but he mightn't have jumped to so corny a conclusion. I laughed and thought: What's the *use*? Experience indeed! We were meant to be so *predictable*; conditioned to scuffle for notice, worry about careers, and have 'experiences'; our fangs drawn before they'd even started to grow. I preferred to wander about and listen to the slow drip of my own boring, undiagnosable wound.

I didn't have this tutor all the time. For Anglo-Saxon I had another, whose patience and accuracy were beautiful to watch. The subject itself was dullness itself and he never succeeded in teaching me more than the rudiments of it, but I admired him so much I tried to copy his precision. His humbleness before his subject – even our lazy stumblings he listened to attentively, they might throw some light on a textual difficulty – gave him a completeness and a dignity I had come to Oxford hoping to admire. He was the only man that I found there who possessed it. In some ways a mouse-like, private person, he was more or less ignored by the other dons.

But that completeness is in the stones. Oxford really has a *genius loci* of great power, which I began to feel. It is the perfect example of a place that is greater than the sum of the people inside it. Many of the dons use this force to shore up themselves – becoming imitation landed-gents or club-men; but the place carries them along with it, a little distance anyway, and even the most recalcitrant undergraduate is somewhat changed. It isn't possible to spend three years inside those walls without emerging a little less brutish than before.

My tutor with his veiled apologies about the weekly essay was only trying to keep in step with the presiding genius of the place. His petulance when taken at his word gave the show away; nevertheless he'd been compelled to try.

A small example of this infecting gentleness: towards the end of our second year we had to attend a ceremony with a Latin name that I forget. (Dons cling to mediaeval Church formulae that the Protestant in them would repudiate immediately if translated into English.) Our work and our characters were to be summed up by dignitaries of the College. I guessed it to be a monastic survival, the Abbot gingering up the novices. I'd been out late and I overslept. I was woken by the Dean. 'We've been waiting for twenty minutes,' was all he said. I pulled on some clothes and ran down to the Senior Common Room; I'd forgotten my tie and gown, the expression on the college butler's face accurately mirrored my appearance, he flung open the door and I stumbled in, eyelids stuck together. They were all there in the sunny, wood-panelled room, ranged along a green-covered table: the Dean, my Tutor, my Moral Tutor (whom I'd never met) and in the centre the Warden. They had the whole of my year to do that day, quarter of an hour each; they'd been sitting waiting for me for half an hour and the Warden never mentioned it.

'Ah! Mr Kavanagh. . . . We have been discussing you . . . and we are all agreed. Your work has been good . . .' (my work? I hadn't done any . . .) 'and although you are unlikely to gain First Class Honours – so much of your time being devoted to other pursuits – we nevertheless feel the way you are spending your time here is extremely sensible and valuable.' After more in the same vein I was dismissed with smiles and nods and went out stunned. Well . . . ! I'd come up two years before with it in my soul to be rude to everybody. The world seemed to me a hateful and lunatic place and in this bourgeois stronghold I wasn't going to pretend otherwise. Since then I'd skimped my work – my 'other pursuits' consisted largely in doing what I pleased – the Warden himself must have seen me pushing a girl over the garden wall at eight o'clock in the morning while he walked past us with an abstracted air. And yet he'd meant what he said. . . . Faced with such tolerance, the kind you hope for all your life and which, like most people, I'd never come across, it was difficult to be a bear. Here at last was something to love, perhaps.

·

But the rotting disease of Oxford is nostalgia. Everything is so obviously there, you have only to reach out and take it, and the time passes so quickly you can regret its passing even before it has arrived. I met people in their first year whose eyes were holes of sadness at the thought of their eventual going down; and there are some who never do, or not for years, returning each weekend like ghosts, staring at the new faces with pale uncomprehending eyes. It affects everyone in some way, even the dons, treading water in an eternally changing river of youth, and they sometimes make a cult of it – falling in love with half-broken voices floating across the gardens in some Shakespearean production (for example). Never mind if the production is bad and the acting absurd so long as it evokes . . . something. I don't know what, the Greek Anthology maybe. It is reflected in the Latin names for the ceremonies and in the ceremonies themselves which have sometimes emptied of all meaning, a respect for tradition that is like a fear of time. And yet it's possible they're right to look after Oxford this way – its power is like the beauty of a certain kind of girl, impossible to say exactly what it consists in, take one imperfection away and the whole may crumble. T. S. Eliot came briefly to my college as a postgraduate student from the States. He left almost at once, I'm told, declaring that he didn't like being dead. If this is true it strikes me as an unusually silly thing for that prematurely agèd eagle to say. I suppose he meant academically, and certainly the Eng. Lit. School is moribund (almost, it would seem, on purpose, to give English the respectability of a dead language). But Oxford is more than an academy, a programme of dreary, inaudible lectures contemptuously delivered, 'gentlemanly' tutorials, textual cruces, and South African sherry. Oxford as an Idea is very alive indeed.

There is a kind of wooziness that creeps into descriptions of Oxford. And if all the colleges were pulled down and rebuilt to look like, say, Balliol, none of this would remain true, so obviously it's in the old buildings. New ones built with the old spirit would work. This exists but not in sufficient quantities. I have no doubt that Oxford is doomed and there's no point in being sorry about that, but the power that is left is effective, and worthy of love. You can hate it too, this oldness, this leftover power (for the 'closed' nature of the circuit which can be thought of as antagonistic to certain kinds of life, though I don't think it is, to any) but it isn't possible to deny it altogether.

Above all there is nothing soft or archaising about this; the true Oxford would be the first to acquiesce in its own dissolution the moment it has lost all meaning. It has seen plenty of violence; it has survived the long porcine slumbers of the eighteenth century, and the architecture of the nineteenth. It has survived countless generations of dons.

For example: the garden of my college, an enclosed Chaucerian bower of green, with grassy banks of crocuses, huge bushes of white lilac, cabbage-roses, and a James the First mulberry tree; it was a camp during the Civil War and later a place of resort for prostitutes; it has seen at least one execution. Its sweetness is of the world, hasn't been cultivated in a vacuum from which all jarring elements have been excluded; whereas the peculiar danger of misunderstanding Oxford is to regard beauty, peace, as somehow dependent on the idealised past alone, waning, fading even while you watch. Rooted in the past certainly (what isn't?) but this kind of sighing nostalgia has dangerous black thumbs because, unlike green fingers, it can make nothing grow. The demand of Oxford is not a precious celebration of youthfulness or, for that matter, ancientness. Oxford, on the contrary, like beauty itself, of which it has so much, is tough. Years later I wrote a poem about Merton garden in which I tried to express this and called it *A particular garden, particularly.*

> *These walls infect the air*
> *with pale nostalgia.*
> *See, through the garden comes*
> *that languished Lady under whose black thumbs*
> *our past grows waxen fruit*
> *our present cannot eat,*
> *and fades, and dies.*
>
> *Listen (and argue); she never says, but sighs*
> *'Stone upon stone well and truly laid*
> *in a noble manner now forgotten . . .'*
> *(the stones themselves are rotten)*
> *'Tops of the trees ruffle like sleeping birds.*
> *A bitter generation has no words*
> *to consecrate the meaning of this garden.'*
>
> *Well then, let us on this meaningful,*
> *ancient, uncomfortable,*
> *breeze-petalled seat,*
> *catalogue some things She misses out.*

Cemented boles.
Rusted iron chains and poles
that prop
Her tattered Lears, Her bird-cage lime-trees up . . .

Under their branches, up and down
the beat now sacrosanct to dog with don
once patrolled the Ladies of the Town . . .

As you carefully lean on the pox of the parapet,
think of the poet Collins taken for debt,
exactly, historically, there, just under it,
drunk in the afternoon . . .

Where Her false-gentle memory glides,
kissing smooth corners (which are not),
is roughly four yards from the spot
where poor Colonel Windebanke,
for giving way to undue funk
at the sight of Ironsides,
one paint-fresh morning such as this
by some outraged friends of his
was brought and shot . . .

No need to go on.
The Lady's gone.

A cow in the Meadows blows her horn
across the liquid green.
Were it not for milking time
no cow, no grass, no water-colour scene.

Lady, agreed this silence
is solace, but You must confess the violence
blending us together;
past, present, future,

calm beauty, rough weather.
Not one without the other.

•

I found the story about Colonel Windebanke in Carlyle. He had some ladies staying with him and they implored him not to resist Cromwell's cannon. The perfect host, he did as they wished, only to discover that crafty old Ironsides hadn't any cannon anyway and could easily have been driven off. Later, as the war moved from the neighbourhood, his comrades decided to make an example of him and put him in front of a firing squad against Merton wall.

I felt this at the time but wrote it in Java three or four years later not in Oxford which to my way of thinking is no place to write verse in. It lends itself too easily in the wrong way – with its sweet-smelling libraries, leisure, shelter, the chatter of oneself and one's friends; its yellow, melancholy autumn evenings; springing, green, bird-singing summers. This is pleasure, this is fun and helpful, but poetry's written in spite of, as well as because.

I was more or less in love most of the time. When each episode came to an end I said goodbye firmly and unsentimentally; on to the next. In this way I think I seriously hurt someone, but I thought it better to face facts than be burdened with false sentiment. I make myself shudder.

Acting took more and more of my time. But I couldn't involve myself in the acting world of the University, where the in-fighting for position and authority struck me, in such circumstances, as blasphemous. I was still guilty about the whole acting business. It seemed too easy, too undemanding. Oxford, as well as everything else, can be a microcosm of the outside world of prestige and competition, and within it acting brought me a ration of Oxford's equivalent of fame, power and the love of women. Having these I could afford not to compete, but I knew that without them, in obscurity, I would have eaten out my heart. This struck me as despicable; it still does, but one learns to live with oneself.

·

Soon it was my last year and there was nothing to do but read Chaucer and Shakespeare. Imagine! The luck of it! Four-fifths of English literature could be destroyed without anyone noticing the loss, but these two made you gasp as they phrased the thoughts you were just beginning to have. You didn't use them as a kind of spring-board, put the book down and dream the rest. You read what they said and they carried you to a world that existed outside yourself and you had a part in that world, you weren't any longer alone; other men had felt what you felt, and more. I locked my door and read like a maniac; I couldn't get enough of it – wished I'd started before but how could I have, it had only just happened?

·

And now something else happened – the point of all this.

The curtain between me and the natural world felt too heavy. It needed a miracle to shift it, to help me recognise another human face; and the miracle came. Or rather she did. She did it – another human being in shoes and gloves and earrings and a past history in which I had no part; she recognised me.

·

I was in digs now, locked away, but the other lodgers had streams of visitors up and down the stairs past my door. None of these disturbed me except one girl who went 'Pom pom POM' as she ran up to the room above. It was a sound of extraordinary sweetness, musical, soft, unselfconscious and happy. I began to listen out for it, jump up from my table, throw open the door to catch a glimpse of her as she passed, but I was always too late. I asked the people upstairs who she was, described the beautiful sound she made. They

became rather guarded and exchanged glances and hesitat-
ingly admitted it just might be Sally. I gathered she was
someone special, not to be discussed in the ordinary way,
and became vaguely curious to meet her. But the last thing
I wanted at that stage was to get involved with anybody. I'd
just come to the end of a satisfactorily painful affair with a
professional dons' girl (one met dons' girls at Oxford just as
one met Officers' girls in the Army.) This one collected threats
of suicide and of broken marriages from the younger tutors
like Girl Guides collect badges – she wore them on her sleeve.
She was also great fun. It had been tempestuous and poign-
ant in a way that was satisfactory to both of us and I considered myself to have suffered. Now, I had work to do.

·

One day I came face to face with a girl on the landing. It
was certainly her, whoever made that noise had to look as
she did. We stood and stared at each other too long for
comfort. I broke the moment and, excusing myself, moved
past her because it was too like the movies, or so I thought
to myself of that long, silent stare, and laughed. She was
tall and proud-looking with a slight round-shouldered stoop
that made me breathless, I didn't know why.

It is difficult to describe someone who is surrounded by a
special nimbus, perceived at once. But as this girl had the
same effect, in one way or another, on many others, I must
try. She had soft yellow hair, greeny-blue eyes, lovely eye-
brows below a broad, quiet forehead and the most perfect
mouth I have ever seen; underneath her skin there were
golden lights. I am not a good physiognomist, I find it dis-
torts a face to see it in detail, and I imagine the peculiar,
extraordinary charm of her face lay in its proportions and in
its expression. When I first saw the friezes in the museum
on the Acropolis I couldn't believe it, most of the girls are

portraits of her. Her face, and above all her expression, belonged to the same ideal, golden time. But beautiful girls are, in a sense, two a penny. There was something even more arresting, something unique in her face. She had the simplicity of a young girl (she was nineteen) who found life good; but it was a simplicity that had somehow been earned, was, as it were, on the second time round. This second simplicity has the directness and potency of a natural force. She had the kind of beauty that can change but not diminish – it depended for so much of its power on the kind of person she was that it could only end when she did. One trembled for her (it was too good to survive) and was humbled at the same time, by a face that was more strongly alive than anyone else's, which contained an indestructible, fearless happiness. She shone.

A few days later we met at a small party and I stood at her side. We didn't speak much. I told her of the noise she made as she passed my door. And often on the days that followed when I got back to my room I found the words 'Poop, poop poop' written on a piece of paper lying on my table – her phonetic spelling of the noise I hadn't been there to hear. One night we made part of a party that went to the theatre together. This entailed her staying the night out of her college and I found her a room in the house where I was living. After saying goodnight I went upstairs back to my desk, I had an essay to write. After a few lines I felt I had to be sure she had everything she needed and went downstairs. She had, and I went back to my work. Another few lines and I knew it was no use. I went down again and she seemed to be waiting for me, her face luminous and amused. I did what I should have done days before, I took her in my arms and kissed her; every experience, however simple, has its maximum brilliance. This happens only once, and is so startingly different from anything less than itself that it seems to contain indications of a strength and a joy far beyond it, a hint that we live only on the edges of a possibility.

I fought and struggled and kicked. I wasn't ready, not for this, not now. I gathered she came from the *haute bourgeoisie* – her mother Rosamond Lehmann, the novelist – her father's father a lord. I had no money, my father had no money, and I hadn't the slightest intention of trying to earn any. I wanted to wander some more and find myself: I didn't want to get mixed up with people like that. Also I had no intention of being caught up in all the flummeries of love, about which I'd read so much that was always suspiciously vague and religiose. I wanted to use my mind, not be trapped in a gust of unspecific dismays and exaltations by a blonde princess I couldn't take my eyes off. I had fighting to do.

I had to admit she had none of the mannerisms or pre-suppositions of her class – in fact was less of a snob than I was myself. Nor was this the protected beauty's ignorance of how the world was made. Her incredulous hatred of in-justice was far more immediately practical than my own – when she could she acted, without hesitation – her father was a Communist, and she once said, she wasn't his daugh-ter for nothing. Nor was she rich, she had the same amount of money as I had. Nevertheless . . . I spent hours in my room explaining to her in so many words, as darkness slowly fell outside, that it was all impossible, without ever defining quite what. And then I'd realise with a spasm of relief that watching me attentively as I strode about she wasn't listening to a word I said but hearing all she wanted to hear revealed in the tone of my voice.

A crust was falling from my surface; the layer of muscles under the skin seemed to be losing their tensions – like waking from a deep sleep they were fresh and elastic and eager for use. I saw her face as it really was. For the first time I was looking at a person outside myself. It was as though my arms, instead of being locked protectively across my chest, were opening out, exposing what I was and what I wanted to be. If I was a dancer I could dance that feeling. I continued to work, with new energy in fact. Far from coming in between, her face lent further colour and meaning to what I had just been beginning to understand. I began to write, and for the first time finish, poems. There was some point in finishing them now – I had her to show them to.

In the Christmas vacation I got myself a job sorting mail. Sally, with the juggernaut simplicity and directness that were her most astonishing qualities, found work at the same Post Office.

When you post things they go down a chute and bounce against a wooden door. Every so often a sack is hung under the door, door opened, contents of chute fall into sack. I was the man who opened the door – Sally was one of the people who lugged away the heavy result. I tried to change places with her, but Post Office regulations wouldn't allow it; so I sat at the bottom of my chute with two retired postmen who besought me not to work so hard and to go and have a cup of tea. I crept out sometimes to watch her, already the centre of the other workers; as always, immediately, perfectly at home. Once I left work a little before she did, and waiting for her on London Bridge I watched her walk down Borough High Street surrounded by her new friends, laughing, all of them jostling to be near her. I felt a stab of jealousy and possessiveness and fear. If she had had eyes only for me I would have left her. But if I should lose her now. . . . And yet I hadn't the guts to say I wanted her. I bought her a sixpenny bunch of violets and against her skin they seemed to burn with a dark blue flame, the drops of moisture on them shining like her eyes.

I wish I could be more specific – give a gesture of hers, or a piece of talk. But she eludes me, as though she's none of my business, and neither is what happened at that time, or later. I find I'm tiptoeing round her now just as I did then, with the same involuntary silence.

They were less afraid of going at such things head-on in the eighteenth century.

'She was tall, well-made, with a candid air and a modest bearing; there was in her face, which was both beautiful and charming, and in all her movements, a mingled sweetness and pride that announced a celestial soul.'

Exactly. So Louvet, hiding from the Terror in his filthy well, remembers Charlotte Corday. Everything he says of her is equally true of Sally, which is what is wrong with it maybe. We see what he means but we don't see a particular girl; no one is as perfect or as abstract as that. But I think when we come across real strength, gentleness, passion, beauty, our comparisons fail us and we do fall silent; such things just are. A silence like that is hard to communicate, which is what is wrong with books, but they're the best we have.

She was beautiful, certainly, and tall and fair. But the most astonishing thing about her appearance, and somehow the first indication of what she was, were those gold lights underneath her skin. They went out sometimes, of course, when she was tired or ill or baffled. And then she was infinitely touching, like a glorious bird in the wet.

·

She asked me to come with her for a couple of days at her father's farm. With an air of detachment I was finding difficult to preserve, I went, carried along by a powerful river that was bearing me further and further towards experiences for which I had no attitudes prepared. I could step back on to the bank any time, but while on the water I could only make a pretence of trying to steer.

Wogan, Sally's father, lived alone at this time; his second wife had died a few months previously and the small white-washed farmhouse was full of brightly coloured rugs and quilts and designs, simple, useful, beautiful things she had made. Wogan was a working farmer but his own paintings were hung in the farmhouse kitchen; strong, mystical land-scapes, and figures working in the fields, gongs and squares of glowing red and brown and yellow. Resistant as I was, I had never imagined a place where everything was so exactly right, so simple and so personal.

This was my first sight of the Cotswolds, the huge sweeping fields, the knotted thorn hedges at the top of high banks, the immense sky. The yellow stone of the farmhouse seemed to have a honey-light inside it, stored from summer. Everything glowed. And looking covertly into Sally's dazzling face as we walked across the fields through the snow, I wondered if it was possible after all to be simple and happy and free.

.

The problem of how to pay for such a life was one I was grateful not to have to face for another six months. But simple and happy and free? It was the central question. My parents, like most parents I suppose, were made uneasy by such speculations and I didn't need them to tell me that such a life required a special kind of nerve. The admiration accorded to getting on with it, to pulling oneself together, seemed to me the self-congratulation of the inmates of a prison to whom everything glimpsed through the bars was immoral or impossible or cheating. But what if it wasn't necessary to go to prison at all?

The Catholicism I'd been taught, for example, was too often negative; a denial of pleasure without a noticeable love of anything greater than pleasure to give it purpose and warmth. So it seemed that people were even more afraid to be happy than they were of being miserable, and I felt this in myself. How absurd to settle for second-best because it would hurt less if that were taken away!

I gave myself up completely to the astonishing pleasure of Sally's company. Joy became a possibility when she was there, it hung like a great golden ball, to be had for the asking. I went to ground and watched it grow and glow until it poured warmth and light into every cranny of my life. I also watched, with wonder, Sally's effect on others. A film came off their faces, subtly transforming their appearance; it was as though people only had to be in the presence of someone they trusted to become quite different, simple, like the soldiers when they talked of their particular friend, as though the laws of evolution, of survival, were suspended once there was no need to compete or perform; in the presence of someone without envy or malice people became transparent and lovable. I'd think: but really he's a sod – when it was clear that though he might very well be that, seen for a moment through Sally's eyes he was also nothing of the kind.

This is a very great embarrassment for a young man, it fills him with a benevolence that is like confusion, makes impossible the clear distinctions and enjoyable indignations that he longs for. Sally could have the same effect on very great crooks and snobs as she had on others that I thought had a greater right to her attention; her simplicity was indifferent, and therefore to me a mystery. There was nothing vague in all this, no *glissando* on the harp-strings, it was perfectly measurable, though we lack the instrument. There are some people whose purity of personality is intact from the cradle, like a magnetic needle they always point in the same direction. The world rearranges itself round them, east, west and south, and as they expect to find it so it becomes. Nor was there anything bromidic: attracted to angular, violent people, their violence was not diminished; people became more, not less, themselves. Needless to say she was unaware of all this.

It's always necessary to probe for the flaw, the mocking other side, to make up the balance. Too much rubbish is talked by those who don't. But to be in the presence of someone who always rings clear, even when you don't understand, is an incredible astonishment. I decided that only time could make me believe my ears.

·

The final examinations were approaching and I had to think about a job. Some of my acquaintances were making regular pilgrimages to the Oxford University Appointments Board, and although I had misgivings about any job based on privilege to the extent of being kept in reserve for Oxford undergraduates, I reckoned my need was as great as theirs and joined the queue.

The Board was a cross little man behind a large desk who dealt out brochures of the large firms like a croupier. His frequent references to pension schemes were a gruesome reminder of one definition of reality and of how permanent the choice was expected to be. Not only did some firms favour 'Oxford men' (as opposed to 'Cantabs' as he jocularly assured me), there were even some who preferred their fodder from a particular college – for all I know there were others who chose their junior executives after consulting the entrails of crows. He sorted out a few who favoured Merton men and asked me if there was anything I particularly wanted to do. At that moment nothing so much as to get out of his office, so I took the scrap of paper he wanted me to fill in and forgot all about it.

The time passed and nothing turned up (I can't imagine what I expected to) so I remembered the scrap of paper, filled it out, sent it in, and was summoned again to the shrine.

He was even crosser this time: 'You do know that first impressions are what count?' I did know, it was a mindless piece of ju-ju I didn't rate highly. However, this was clearly one of those interviews that is concerned with an unconsciously committed crime so I said 'Yes' to hear what came next: the length of my hair? Or the fact that someone had put a thunderflash in my duffel-coat pocket on Guy Fawkes night and blown half the side out of it?

'This form you've filled in and sent me . . . I cannot abide any form of bigotry! This country of ours happens to have an *Established Religion*! And it happens to be called the *Catholic* religion! Why then have you put Catholic in the space marked religion, when it is obvious that you meant ROMAN Catholic?' By this time he was waving my form about as though it was burning his fingers. 'SOME people might take great offence at this!'

This was all news to me. No cradle-Catholic ever calls himself 'Roman'. But if Non-Roman Catholics didn't use any adjective, how had he known that I didn't mean what I'd said – Catholic, i.e. Church of England? However, I was enjoying his hatred of bigotry too much to argue.

He simmered down and began impatiently to deal out the pack of brochures again. I stopped him before I burst into tears and broke it to him as gently as I could that what I really fancied was somewhere warm where they paid a living wage and there wasn't too much work. He suddenly became a very old man, his head sunk into his shoulders – dragging a weary hand across his face he gestured weakly with his spectacles for me to leave him. As I tiptoed towards the door he groaned into his blotter: 'Try the British Council.' So I did.

I tracked down a professor who wanted temporary assistants at the British Institute in Barcelona for a year. He was a jolly cove, temporary himself, sweating slightly under the formalities of Davies Street, and looked as though he needed a drink; as I left the room I had the impression he gave me a wink as the officials around him bent their noses to the file of the next candidate. I wasn't sure but maybe I had a chance of that job.

But it wouldn't begin till September – it was now June. Sally was in Italy with her mother. I didn't want to spend that time in London, with my parents; nor, I am sure, did they want me to. They were so happy together in many ways, I often felt gooseberry.

Casper Wrede, a young Scandinavian director, was forming a theatrical company, partly professional, partly undergraduate, to appear at the Edinburgh Festival. He asked me to play Mortimer in Marlowe's *Edward II*, so the problem was solved.

.

We lived in the Recreation Hall for Corporation Dustmen in Advocates' Close in the Royal Mile, the slums of Edinburgh. Hogg had stayed in that Close, so had Boswell; and at the end of the narrow wynd where we rigged up our canteen Burke and Hare had murdered Bonny Mary Patterson. I loved that dark, festering area, a stews since the eighteenth century – stinking of violence and history. I loved the warmth of the local people and the work itself, rehearsing a good play under an intelligent director, and the sense of community. It was astonishing, the selflessness of human beings, when they're convinced that what they're doing is worth while, and no one is taking advantage of them. I'd noticed it in the Army, it was in the love the soldiers showed. Not only did the café owners, poor enough God knows, often refuse payment and press huge double-helpings on those of us they reckoned needed 'building up', but some of our own helpers, living in rat-infested cellars (one girl had her ear chewed by a rat while she was sleeping but wouldn't complain), did hard boring work for months and for no reward. I couldn't imagine this happening in the firms with the glossy brochures. It seemed there was a central, simple nerve in everyone – press it and Hey presto! the prison bars swung open, melted away. The problem was to find the nerve in oneself, and having found it, never to let it go. Everything else was merely a waiting for death.

A letter came from the professor, I'd got the job.

·

Why, when I was so happy, did I leave Sally and go to Spain for a year? There were so many reasons, and looking back I still find most of them good ones. I wanted to find out what I felt. When we're young we really don't know, not clearly; we feel so many things all at once, they have to be disentangled. Love, what is love, we read so much about it, Love? Was what I felt for Sally this? She burned inside me, casting a glow, but round the edges it was dark and battles were fought there so noisily I couldn't hear myself think. And there were practical reasons. Sally still had a year to do at Oxford. If I hung around doing some dismal job, living at home, getting more and more beaten, saving the fare to go down sometimes for weekends while she played out her old, gay life – I knew myself – I'd become sulky, suspicious, demanding; I'd spoil everything. If I'd had any money I would have stayed – there's an economic root to most things – but the absence of it, keeping us apart, altering everything, would have made me savage; I preferred to be absent myself.

Why didn't I become an actor, when all the pointers pointed that way, the only thing I'd shown myself to be any good at? I thought and thought about it: even went for a half-hearted interview about a job in Redcar. I suppose like most complexities it can be reduced to a simplicity for practical purposes. I didn't because I didn't want to. I wanted to be a poet.

At the Air Terminal Sally let fall the one small bitterness I ever heard from her. She was right; there was no glossing over what I was doing; I was leaving her, and I shouldn't have been. For the first time I felt that garotte tightening round my throat – pulled on one side by the lack of money, on the other by the need to do something stupid to earn it. I knew what I wanted: to live with Sally, and explore the world; but I didn't see how. Perhaps the real reason I went away was because, like many another, I didn't know what else to do.

AFTER THE USUAL initial period of dismay –
what am I doing here? – I found myself a room slightly less
horrible than the others I'd looked at. One black-bombazined
widow had offered me the bed her husband had died in four
days previously, it was still laid out like a bier beneath a livid
crucifix, bleeding after the Spanish fashion. She haggled res-
olutely through her tears.

I found Spanish, or perhaps I should say Catalan, interiors
to be in the Victorian presbytery waiting-room style. They
always looked as though the inhabitants lived elsewhere.
Huge chandeliers that came to rest a few inches above the
antimacassared dining-table, heavy, black oaken chairs like
instruments of torture, and on the walls dark religious pictures, sentimental and blood-soaked at the same time. The
shutters were always drawn, and although everything was
over-clean it was all coated with an unhealthy clinging silence, worse than dust. You instinctively lowered your voice;
I found myself conducting the negotiations in whispers, my
heart in my boots.

These were the apartments of the embattled middle class,
and perhaps one of the necessary expressions of a régime
the chief supporters of which seem to be the old women and

priests. The flats are huge because they're designed to a celibate clergy's ideal of family life – three generations under one roof – a horrible thought. The men either clear out altogether or take their pleasures elsewhere, leaving the women to preside balefully over echoing caverns of mahogany, as though keeping them in readiness for the laying out of a corpse.

Spaniards seldom entertain at home, but the few times I was invited home by pupils, some of them middle-aged men still living with their mothers, there was usually this heaviness, this suffocating ugliness, the absence of light and air, the dreadful, empty ceremoniousness without grace or style. And my host out of respect, and for all I knew, love, for his mother, paid lip-service to her narrow, cruel views: a woman of no experience, no reading, whose only point of contact was the clergy whom he affected to despise.

My room was very dark, and made darker by wallpaper patterned in intricate shades of dung. However it had a bed, a chair and a narrow table from which each day I moved the lace doily and put my notebook there instead. Each night I found the notebook put away, the doily replaced. The ornaments I removed and returned to my landlady saying that I was afraid I might break them. This she understood and clutched them to her accusingly, as though in fact I had. She was a woman of curious habits. The flat divided into two, with the lavatory on the landing in between. Every time I used it, whatever time of day or night, there would be a pause, and then a furtive shuffle of slippers and she'd go in there; a few minutes later I'd hear the plug being pulled again. This filled me with a peculiar kind of horror. Once, in the early hours, I looked up from my book and saw her shadow outlined on the wall – she was somewhere out in the hall, watching me. The shadow stayed there for perhaps quarter of an hour, quite still, and then it went away. I can only add that these lodgings were the least sinister I'd been able to afford.

I wasn't paid very much, but the work was pleasant and gave me time to do my own. I settled down in earnest to learn my trade – in a way I now think mistaken, if not absurd. I took Yeats' words as my text but tried so hard to make my verses 'well made' that I jammed up whatever lyricism I might have had left. I was so terrified of being dilettante that the end-result was often professional in the worst sense, although the original impulse was perhaps simple, and strong. I became obsessed with the idea of getting into print; this would give me professional status in my own eyes. I sent a long poem, very Audenesque and called *St Thomas More* to John Lehmann. I had misgivings about this, I didn't want to be published because I knew his niece, but he was the best literary editor at the time and hadn't struck me as the sort of man who would publish anything he didn't like. I was quite right and he didn't. I plugged on, turning out reams of stuff, trying to get Auden out of my system.

Some years later I was talking to a famous editor about the exciting experimental work in American magazines. 'Ah yes,' he cried, thumping the table, 'but they haven't got anyone to call them to order!' I wish I hadn't called myself to order so much.

But I knew that poetry was a way of life as well as an acquired skill. Maybe the age didn't want you, but nevertheless your temperament, however poor a thing, was needed, whether others knew this or not. The job was to find a means of existence (a job) that kept this temperament functioning. Let the poems come or not come as destiny decided, but your ear had to be cocked to inside noises, and therefore to outside ones as well. I didn't like theorising, however, it made me uneasy. I just burrowed away and three days a week taught English.

Heaven knows if I taught it. I didn't know the answers to most of the questions myself, if indeed there are any, and the lessons filled me with commiseration for those who wanted to learn this impossible language. It was very tiring work, more like a performance. When I was stumped for comedy material I made them do quizzes, like the difference between 'washing down' and 'washing up' (poor sods!) and what they enjoyed most were each other's mistakes. The pupils were mostly girls, and I suppose I showed off, but it seemed better to have the full attention of the class, even if you were talking rubbish, than to be feeding them the real stuff (whatever that might be) and nobody listening. I also took classes outside, old ladies in their drawing-rooms, barmen in their bars; I was saving to get back to spend Christmas in England.

Clifford King, a writer who was also teaching at the Institute, introduced me to the Glorieta, the cheapest restaurant in Barcelona – in the world maybe. If you bought a kind of season ticket your three-course dinner worked out about eightpence; the trouble was you had to be very strong to eat it. Afterwards I filled up a bottle with heavy black wine in the fish-smelling cave of the bar next-door, and went home to work on my poem for Sally's birthday – the wine helping me to forget the dinner.

For lunch I went to the same restaurant every day, near where I worked, had the same meal, and read through the complete back numbers of *Horizon* and *Penguin New Writing*; I'd found them in the Institute library. There I wrote the first poem in what sounded like my own voice. It was my declaration of impatience with a fuzziness I thought I detected in the work of my near-predecessors. I wanted something more specific, colder, tougher, and I felt that I was hoisting a standard of revolt. In fact it was only a bit of Kleenex pinned to a stick, but it was a beginning. I don't think I changed it, but left it as I'd scribbled it down, between the cuban rice and the inevitable *flan*.

Love Poem

Can you forgive the fastidious cannibal
His unusual pleasures? Does your charity
Embrace the noisy whore, forgetting her manners
In front of your daughter? The cocky-walker
Who teaches your wife to care about clothes again
And look in the mirror? And yet defend
Your wife from your enemy and your daughter
From the convincing whore, your life from the cannibal?
When you can do this, and this, and lose
Your wife, your life and always your curious daughter,
Then we may talk of love and what we mean.

I showed it to Clifford and he was very angry about the reference to whores, which he considered disrespectful. Some of the nicest people he'd ever met, and what about Mary Magdalene? Don't tell him Jesus never slept with her, and a good thing too! I had nothing against whores and meant them no harm in my poem.

I've no idea whether Clifford was a good novelist or not because he always told me his plots, in detail, so I didn't need to read the book. I riposted by talking about my feelings for Sally, whom I missed to the point of obsession and, bless him, he listened to it all. A gentle, independent, courageous man, he showed me Barcelona, for which he had a passion. He wrote a good book about it later, called *To Barcelona, with Love*.

First, he introduced me to his friends the whores. In those days there were certain quarters of Barcelona where you could push almost every other door and go upstairs to a room filled with bored girls in transparent shifts, some of them asleep, and a few men reading the evening paper. Every now and then one of these would finish his paper with a sigh, fold it carefully longways, put it in his pocket, glare at one of the girls (often a woman of motherly proportions and advanced years) and jerk his head towards the door. She'd yawn, stretch, and carry on the loud conversation with her colleagues until she was almost in the corridor – then she'd remember her role, dig the customer in the ribs and switch on a lecherous grimace of such cosmic phoniness it was a wonder it didn't freeze him in his tracks. But usually he'd stopped looking at her by this time – thinking of something else probably. It was interesting to see the hot-blooded Latins at play.

This was a fairly high-class one, about ten bob a time. You could pay anything from five quid to ninepence, and there was a separate establishment for every pocket. The walls of the poorest ones were glazed like public lavatories with yellowing, cracked tiles. Exhausted, ill-looking women in greasy Mother Hubbards, their hair hanging down in damp strings, circulated among the crowd, absently rubbing a crutch here and there, eyes empty, trying to raise a spark that would lead a man to spend the pennies he couldn't afford, her share of which would be farthings. One night I saw one of them amusing the other women by pulling out her child-distended nipples as far as they would go, and letting them snap back, like pieces of brown elastic.

In the quieter ones, the seven and six or ten bob ones (God knows these had few enough customers in that poor rich city) Clifford sat and talked with the girls and I admired some of the bodies, wondering at the variety of shapes. Sometimes I got interested, in a pin-up book sort of way, and if only the girls could have acted a little better, or a little less, I mightn't have felt so much like laughing. I felt lust all right, to a burdensome extent, but these girls couldn't have

dispelled it – I'd have to regard either them, or myself, as
less than human. I didn't have the sort of ideal gaiety that
cuts through such things, makes contact. In the first place
their attitude was that of a contemptuous nurse-maid – His
lordship wants his dinner does he? . . . come along then
you. . . . And in the second place these were female human
beings who were trapped – we could walk out of the door
into the world of possibility, these girls stayed here in this
one, as limited as a zoo. Sometimes there'd be a new girl
and she'd sit there looking frightened, and that was horrible.

Clifford got their stories from them, and these were suspiciously often of the 'don't darken my doors again' variety;
and he'd inveigh against the corrupt society that could bring
about such things, and the Church that encouraged it, then
he'd disappear for twenty minutes and emerge stroking his
beard and looking pleased with life; after that we'd go and
pretend to eat the dinner in the Glorieta. I couldn't make up
my mind whether he was exploiting the results of a corrupt
society, or sending money back into the system that would
help alleviate it. Both, I supposed.

Many of the girls were, in fact, unmarried mothers; and
as there is hardly any work for women in Spain, in order to
feed their children they probably had had no choice. In the
mornings they turned the Cosmos bar into a kind of crèche,
and then they'd all sit and say the Rosary together before
the day's work, praying always for a rich husband. These
they sometimes found when the American Navy put into
port. There was a paid scribe in the Cosmos who translated
the sailors' love-letters – passionate avowals from eighteen-
year-olds to 'my pure angel'; and for a fee the scribe com-
posed suitable replies. They were not deceiving these boys,
or no more than other women often do; they obviously
adored them and the future that they made possible. I don't
know what happened when the sailors found out, but I'm

sure some of those girls made marvellous wives, though probably fiercely respectable.

But always this terrible, crushing poverty. There was an old woman with ulcerated legs outside the Cosmos bar with three lemons in front of her. She wasn't begging, but I never saw her sell one; how on earth did she eat? The money seemed to have settled at the top, like scum. The rich were too rich and they knew it, it poisoned them. The air was thick with hate. Stopped by a policeman for jumping a traffic-light, the owner of a car that cost more than most of the pedestrians would earn in their lives shouted at the policeman that he'd make him lose his job, and he stepped back and saluted; this was normal. But it was no use a foreigner being safely indignant when the Spaniards themselves kept so quiet. They were not apathetic, but they knew the cost better than we did.

.

Barcelona is built on the grid system – the street plan looks like a schoolboy's empty stamp-album – and bisecting the whole city is the Avenida Generalisimo Franco; this is a name seldom mentioned in separatist Catalonia so the street is always called, accurately, the Diagonal. Above it, up the hill towards the dominating mountain, Tibidabo, live the rich – I lived there myself – and these seldom venture more than a few blocks across it except to go to the opera and there they get out of their cars quickly, looking neither right nor left, talking loudly to each other in the middle of the small, silent crowd that always gathers. Below the Diagonal the city gets progressively poorer and more lively; this is where the Ramblas are, the Barrio Chino, the Paralelo with its dozens of music-halls, and at the very bottom is the sea.

Each of the bars in the Paralelo specialises in one kind of regional music, Basque, Galician and so on. They are as I imagine the *cafés chantants* to have been in nineteenth-century

Paris – noisy, vigorous and talented. And there were proper music-halls where for the price of a drink you could sit and listen to a succession of hugely vital Marie Lloyds belting out songs and back-chatting with the roaring audience. They had the steely, Spanish voices that can shatter glass, hoarding-sized personalities in perfect accord with their audience, a suggestion of the vast forces that lay just under the surface: the reservoirs of energy and strength that were being wasted.

My middle-class friends never set foot in this area, some even affected to doubt its existence. They lived behind their walls, each of them with his atrocity story of the Civil War; pictures ripped apart, books and carpets wantonly destroyed, relatives murdered. They looked to Paris and London for their culture and Germany for their business: they felt they lived in a backwater and ignored the popular culture on their doorstep that in Paris and London had long since passed away.

There were pleasures one degree more sophisticated. If you walked through the Bohemia grocery and bent under the hanging sausages you came to a door that led to a cellar in which, twice nightly, Madame Clara and le grand Gilbert held court. Madame Clara was a huge woman with goitrous eyes and a toppling scarlet wig who sang selections from Grand Opera in the style of Madame Flora Jenkins. She had no voice at all, just squeaked and screamed, but was well satisfied with the noise she made and bowed graciously to the applause. If anyone laughed she stopped and stared the philistine into confusion, and so did the rest of us. Le grand Gilbert was a delightful old queen of about ninety who archly chortled songs that had been risqué fifty years before, and then, with a charmingly coy expression that said: 'we're all friends here so let's go just a weeny bit too far' he'd don a wig and pulling his trousers above his thin, varicosed calves gave us his imitation of Mistinguett. Cruel perhaps to enjoy it so much, but I don't think so. Their fantasy was so complete. Our private ones in the audience were just as strong, but not so perfect.

A painter I knew was learning the guitar from a gypsy. We went to listen to him playing for coins among his own people down by the docks; dark barrels piled up on the sawdust floor, scraggy chickens picking about among the cigarette ends and the spat-out olive stones. One night three dark Andalusians came in, workmen far from their southern home, tired and drunk. They stood at the bar, swaying a bit, and softly the one in the middle began to sing – the thin, scarcely human notes of the South. His body became rigid; the noise, coming from somewhere deep in his throat, rose in pitch and volume and the bar fell quiet. He bent himself further and further back as though trying to make his body a tube the sound could flow through and his companions supported him. He was making the noise we all make sometimes at the back of our heads, but turned to music, poured out and shown to us. Slowly the marvellous, vibrating crying faded, the muscles and veins on his stretched neck subsided; he straightened himself and picked up his glass. What he had done he had done for himself. Conversation started up again.

Two of the guitar-playing gypsy's friends came over. They lived in the *barracas*, the dreadful shanty-town built of old packing-cases on the outskirts of the city. One of them had his arm in a grey sling which had a green and yellow stain on it, crusted with pus. After a stately introduction he withdrew from the deep interior of the sling a half-smoked cigarette, presenting it to me with a bow. It was a gesture of hospitality, regal, simple and very generous. It was almost certain that cigarette represented his whole wealth for the evening.

This was what people came to Spain to find: the music,

the pride. . . . And we sat there distinguishing between various kinds of purity, all of them arising out of a poverty we did not share.

The painter who showed me this side of Barcelona was a New Zealander and I was told (as one always is) that he had said of me that I had a 'horizon of cabbages'. (Incidentally I have never met an Australian, or a New Zealander who didn't heartily detest Englishmen, and thought the Mother Country, Queen and Commonwealth, etc., a load of old codswallop just as I do. Does it then exist?) In a way I think he was right. These excursions into other people's lives made me uneasy though not, I imagine, in the way he thought. To pretend to be one of them, for a couple of hours a night, was a lie. The eighteenth-century milord savouring the picturesque didn't give himself the brotherhood-of-man kick as well; he was in the stalls and they were in the dust and that was how he liked it – that was also the way it was. To be alive you had to be more involved than you could afford. The marshy swamp inside me was beginning to turn into a river that flowed in one direction: and Sally was not a row of cabbages.

The home-movies flash on the screen and the trapped guests scratch and yawn; self with gypsies, self with whores: sights and sensations acquired like beer-mats – indications of a travelledness, and of a richness gained by travelling – in fact, just beer-mats.

But living abroad there's a chance you may come across someone you wouldn't have met at home, because there you live in your bag, we all do, and at home the bag fits better and we're less aware of it. But this contact with another mind (even abroad it's usually one of our own race, so great is our human constriction) acting in the comparatively associationless arena of a foreign country, may help us to punch a peep-hole or two in the envelope. Collecting experiences is just one way of filling up with unrelated pieces of junk; but a lucky encounter can change the part in us that does the experiencing, change the size of the bag altogether.

Through Clifford, at the Glorieta, I met Pearse Hutchinson.

They didn't like each other much. It was clear that when Clifford spoke of the earthy vitality of the Paralelo music-halls, for example, Pearse at once suspected him of the higher-tourism, the collecting habit that was worrying me. This wasn't quite fair, but they were made not to understand each other. Their confrontation was like a tableau of Anglo-Irish history. Clifford was North Country, an avowed plain man, and when he announced his passion for the King James' Version: 'They knew how to write then! "Lord I believe. Help thou my unbelief" ' – or thumped the table, quoting Tennyson, so that Paco the waiter came running in a spray of sweat: ' "There lives more faith in honest doubt, believe me, than in half your creeds" ' – Pearse couldn't believe his ears. As an Irishman he found Clifford's simplicities barbaric. And Clifford wondered why Pearse didn't wash more.

In Pearse I found one of the two or three in a lifetime friends whose judgment I could trust even when he was wrong. His devils of derision screamed quite as loudly as mine, and what he believed and cared for, he did so in their presence. It's a steely and subtle bond that, between two entirely self-conscious people who trust nothing, and yet manage, almost in spite of themselves, to retain a faith in the possibility of much.

He was a poet in a way that delighted and shocked me. He scribbled his poems in bars, and at bus-stops and seldom changed them. The result was always exciting; I'd try to get him to correct a verse (it was easy to see I'd been to Oxford) and he'd agree, but he never did; instead he wrote another poem. His vocabulary was exotic, but not in the tourist-poet sense, if the word was right it went in, whatever language it was; Irish, Castilian, Dutch, even Javanese – I drew the line at *nasih goreng* which is Javanese fried rice and he replied by describing how delicious it was. Not long after I was eating platefuls of it and understood why he insisted on keeping it in.

For the first time I had another professional to show my poems to for criticism, and he responded so generously, accepted me so unquestioningly, that I was able to gauge from the fine shades of his praise just where they were bad. To be perceptively kind about his work is the greatest service one writer can do for another. People often misunderstand this egoism, this eagerness for continual congratulation. I believe it's more often humility than the opposite, and has a technical function. Quite simply, praise is of more practical use than pointing out the faults. In his relief at not having his work rejected outright (at that minute prepared to defend it to the point of absurdity), mollified so much that he can admit to himself it may not be perfect after all – he's set free to criticise himself and if he's any good he'll be able to do that better, and more harshly, than anybody. In fact praise helps him to see where his work is bad, and unlike hostility, which either gets him stuck defiantly in the same groove or shuts him up altogether, it helps him to write more, and differently, and possibly better.

This Pearse did for me, tirelessly, at the same time letting me off nothing. When I showed him a rather phoney exercise called 'Song' he sniffed suspiciously: 'Can you sing it?' Stung, because I hadn't thought of that, I said Yes, and did so. He didn't enjoy the experience much but endured it to the end and then said hastily: 'Well all right then you can sing it.' He wasn't convinced and neither was I.

He was so important to me at this moment (he still is as

a friend but then it was the right man at the right time), I feel like describing him in detail à la Turgenev, starting with his parents. I'll content myself with a sketch. He is perhaps three or four years older than I am. About his appearance the most significant thing to say is that he considers himself ugly. He isn't, but has a large lower lip which he tries to hide by holding an almost too well-shaped hand in front of his mouth, which makes it difficult sometimes to hear what he says. This is a pity because he is the best talker I've met, and the only one I've ever left feeling I was more intelligent than I'd thought. From this it may be gathered that he has perfect manners. Also he has glasses. His walk, seen from afar, is astonishingly springy and eager – gives you the clue to the steely poet's independence under the diffidence, and to the appetite for life. He can distinguish with joy, and precision, between the different types of bread given away with the meal in certain restaurants – and so on through the scale and the day – nothing escapes his vigilance for pleasure, or his indignation.

He is poor, as befits a poet who can leave a richly paid job in the United Nations when required to translate a speech about giving 'wants' to Africans so they are forced into debt and therefore to work more than they need. He has the frequent artist's paranoia that prevents him from showing his work to editors he doesn't know, which allows others to slip into the soggy net of recognition while he swims privately elsewhere. His trousers are sometimes baggy, his collars greasy and if he had any money I suspect he would be a dandy. He regards himself as a coward and I have seen him turn to rebuke a bullfight crowd for their blood-lust. He is regarded by some as lazy and he gives himself no intellectual rest at all. Not surprisingly and not infrequently he drinks too much. It annoys me that not everyone who reads this will know whether what I say of him is true or whether he's worth so much and that I can't decide for certain whether this is his fault or ours.

He didn't bother with caged whores, starving gypsies or Spanish singing and dancing (which the locals regard as African anyway) unless he came upon these naturally; instead he learned the strange, monosyllabic language that twanged around us, sounding as though it consisted of abbreviations. Catalan is the language of a large and prosperous part of Spain, but it is forbidden by the central government to print newspapers in it, or books. This does not apply however to books of poetry and as a result poetry flourishes as nowhere else I've ever been.

The position of the poets is I imagine the same in all police states – critical of aspects of the régime, loving their own country, ungrateful to foreigners who cannot possibly understand this ambivalence and who try to make their cause their own – these also had sole responsibility for an ancient and vital literary culture. Catalan is not the Welsh of Castilian Spain, spoken in country districts out of ignorance and in towns out of bloody-mindedness, it is the language of workmen, and businessmen and contemporary philosophers, and traces directly back to the Provençal of the troubadours. Poets like Blai Bonet, Salvador Espriu and Carlos Riba could stand on their own in any company, but what was particularly exciting was the way in which they, and others, were needed. Ridiculous to say this from so far outside, but there is something very enviable in the situation of a writer whose words have such resonance they put him constantly in danger.

Pearse translated them, as often as possible working over the translations with the poets themselves. We arranged a reading at the British Institute – first the poets read their own work, then we read the translations. The place was crowded out, it was perhaps the first gathering of the kind since the Civil War; public meetings of Catalan writers were forbidden. The bemused Director, astonished I think that poetry could cause so much fuss (the jolly Professor who'd given me the job had almost immediately departed, replaced by a British Council man from Yugoslavia who had left his attention among the Serbo-Croats), embarrassed by the crowd of literates who showed no sign of going home, rummaged in his office cupboard, unearthed an old, half-finished bottle of sherry (legacy of his vanished predecessor), looked again at the couple of hundred people and slipped out the back way. Sherry or no, they stayed for hours, talking in the exuberant, guarded and exploratory manner that is second nature to intellectuals in Spain. I don't know whether anything like it was allowed to happen again.

My own poems were occasionally being printed by now, but I was disappointed how little this meant. The problem was still how to keep in training, like a boxer, only without the punchbags and the skipping-ropes and the date of the big fight not fixed yet.

Sally came out in the spring. When she left I'd walked a good way from the station before it hit me. I had to sit down on a bench. It was impossible to imagine how to get through the rest of the day without her. The sense of loss was overwhelming, physical: quite different from anything I'd experienced before. Every part of me hurt, I couldn't move, so I just sat there, amazed, frightened and somehow overjoyed that any emotion, even pain, could be so huge.

I had no idea what to do, how to pay for being with Sally – however little you needed you needed something. Take a job I supposed, but what? And jobs took up so much time and energy I needed for my own work. I scoured the biographies of other writers to see how they'd managed it, but of course none of their circumstances exactly fitted my own.

I don't know any more why I didn't have her move out to Spain and start from there; I don't know a lot of things.

The bleatings of a young man in this position are not altogether attractive, as he himself knows very well. He stands accused at the same time of preciousness – poor dear's too delicate to go out and get his hands dirty – and self-indulgence – why doesn't he write when he gets back from work and buy his freedom that way? The impatience is justified maybe; as the Man without Qualities says: 'if life is magnificent one cannot ask that it should be easy' – but because a problem presents aspects of feebleness is no reason for pretending it doesn't exist. Men at the end of their lives tend to make either too much or too little of their early struggles, touch them up or tone them down; this is because put baldly they would have a depressing flavour of mere silliness. So be it; early struggles sometimes do, and that's the worst part. A young writer may be determined not to be snuffed out, but he can never be perfectly sure all the time that what he's protecting is worth the trouble. If he had the leisure, would what he wrote be good? Unlike, say, the young physicist, welcomed by society, granted a lengthy, indeed lifelong apprenticeship, the writer has to justify himself straight away or 'get on with it' – and often he can't.

An unattractive dilemma – and I was in it. I'd been given the biggest stroke of luck possible, but the mechanics of building a frame round it stumped me, making me wild with impatience at myself.

I worked out the rest of the contract in Barcelona, turning all this over in my mind, getting nowhere.

Then, one morning, the last piece of clinker fell away, that's exactly what it felt like, or as though I'd just cracked out of a plaster mould.

The moment I'd been waiting for had arrived and it's difficult to describe precisely, or without sounding pretentious, but it comes quite clearly to a certain temperament (I can't speak of others) and presents itself as a choice; is one to live by one's own selection of realities, or that of other people? It can be crudely represented (to avoid talk of leaps into abyss or walks into darkness which nevertheless might contain some truth) by the decision whether to jump on to an escalator (the existence of which is in exact proportion to the extent of your belief in it) or simply to approach the normal stairs in the normal way, one at a time, pausing and looking about. It is in fact a move into the dark for the sake of a possible greater clarity – a gamble. Prudence suggests the jump may be into thin air. Faith, that's to say the trust that places foremost those sudden unclenchings of the heart and nerves, infrequent maybe but nevertheless glimpses of a world of possibility in which reality can be rearranged, within the same limitations, say, as those of a landscape gardener – faith in these redeeming revelations (there are no other words for them) demands that you jump. Really, it depends what sort of world you prefer, and perhaps there's only an illusion of choice. But there is nothing illusory about the moment. I knew perfectly well I was deciding the course of my life, not only in the practical sense, but also the course of my future being. What I had to decide was whether or not I believed enough in the existence of what I wanted.

There is a timing in circumstances that pays no attention to our own personal timing; the ascending golden ball was there to be followed, or to be left until it dissolved into its own attributes, into an experience like any other; this was the moment of equipoise between the two states, so I jumped. I can still hear the slap of my feet on the tiles of the bedroom floor – there was something audible about the whole experience – and I got on the telephone cancelling classes. Any money I'd had in advance I crammed into envelopes and posted back. It left me enough to reach Avignon by which time the last of my pay would have been in England and I could wire for the rest of my fare. I knew exactly what I had to do; go and get Sally before someone else did. Everything else was nonsense even if it was true and if there'd been a wall in the way I could have walked through it. It was the kind of visitation that for the rest of your life you make your acts of faith to. Anything so completely certain is completely true.

SALLY HADN'T BEEN waiting for me, in any overt or self-depreciating way. You don't leave a girl like her for a year, with only a couple of brief meetings in twelve months, and expect to find her knitting socks for you when you come back. She wasn't that kind of chattel at all. But she'd been waiting to see what I'd do.

The emotion of seeing her face again, in the context of such certainty, was not the kind that happens twice in a grown-up lifetime. You know it as a child, when you think you're lost in a crowd; and then you find you're not.

She'd withdrawn a little, but that didn't bother me; I'd come back to a point of rest more demanding than mountain climbing, it was the moving escalator and it would need all I had that was good just to stay in the place I'd reached – a few cubic feet (when we were together) that was my mobile slot in the world – and for it I'd fight at last with everything I'd got, tooth and nail and cunning.

•

During the period that followed I managed to get almost everything to do with external circumstances hopelessly wrong. It was as though I'd used up my ration of being right.

To have regrets runs counter to the sentimental stoicism

of our time. I suppose the ideal twentieth-century man lies on his death-bed vigorously rejecting guilt and announces he would have the whole lot over again and nothing changed. So far I've managed to regret a great deal; at this time I made about every mistake possible, and I wish I hadn't. I was looking, with the conviction of a castrato in a brothel, for a job that I didn't believe existed; one that allowed me enough time to get on with my work. And as far as my practical life was concerned I did feel gelded. I seemed to have exhausted the courage required to ask myself what I really wanted, and so I no longer knew what it was. I was also burdened with the ludicrous ambition, God knows why, to live like everyone else – whatever that may mean.

Television was newish, and expanding, perhaps they could use me. I was interested in documentary films until I realised that was a word that made them shudder in 1955; the only other more taboo was 'fantasy', for which I thought television very suited, but it made them hop about in simulated fury, so great was their fear of seeming highbrow. I did treatments of nonfantastic ideas I dredged up – behind the scenes in the ragtrade – the effect of Polish miners on a Welsh community, and so on. They seemed enthusiastic, sent me away to work the ideas over. I did so – more enthusiasm – I even met the big boss who delivered an impromptu lecture on the Medium (there was much talk of the Medium in those days) which finished up: 'I don't care what it is – *Hamlet* or *I Love Lucy* – the script is télevision' (the pros always call it télevision while the rest of the world says televísion) 'the script is Tee Vee if you can see it – er – see it – er – *visually!* . . . Isn't that so?' Four heads in the room nodded together like metronomes, four pairs of eyes fastened themselves sightlessly on toe-caps or on the ceiling, lost in wonder at the profundity of this thought.

But it was easy to laugh – these men were at least immersed in a job, whereas I was perched on the edge of a chair trying to look useful. To do them justice they were pretty uncertain what they were after and so was I, which must have made me uninspiring to interview; they yawned a good deal.

I did a feature for sound radio on the Pre-Raphaelites. Spent weeks in the British Museum on that, found some interesting stuff and fell in love with Morris. I showed the long-hand draft to a Features producer – more enthusiasm – he stuffed it in his pocket and we went off to celebrate on the strength of it until I had to drop out through lack of cash. When I next succeeded in tracking him down he confessed that at some stage of the celebration after I'd left him he'd lost it.

Money saved in Barcelona was running out, the Pre-Raphaelite script had been the last chance, things were getting desperate. I had a priggish horror of advertising but it paid well. Perhaps I could do it for a year, make enough money to get married and then leave. The application form for J. Walter Thompson's was a huge American affair probing to the depths of your personality; that is to say there were lists of virtues and vices and you had to cross off the ones you had. You were also required to give an autobiography up to the age of ten. I answered all the questions with earnestness (I needed the job) and just to make sure I'd been earnest enough I showed what I'd done to my father. After he'd got over his astonishment at the form he said the answers looked fine to him, so I sent it off. I had a letter back from the Personnel Manager telling me that J. Walter Thompson's did not appreciate flippancy in applicants for employment.

I returned to Portland Place. Surely I could be of some use, for a while anyway, in the Features Department of the B.B.C.? I knew some of the people in it and it wasn't possible

I could be more unemployable than they were. Laurence Gilliam, the head of it, was kind – lent me his book called: 'How to Write Features for Radio.'

All this time my attention was really elsewhere, and it must have showed. Drowsy men bombinating after lunch behind their desks about the Medium of Television, or the Unexplored Resources of Sound Radio – their voices scarcely reached me through the happiness ringing in my ears – I couldn't listen. I just looked at them, vaguely hoping they'd help me, and they listened to themselves.

I was summoned before a B.B.C. Board, one of the members of which was a contemporary from Oxford (my year in Barcelona was catching up with me). Things looked hopeful, characters in pubs in Great Portland Street said: 'Hear you're joining us?' and I saw myself rubbing shoulders with Louis MacNeice, spending three months preparing ten minutes on 'John Clare and His Landscape' or 'Dogs and Thomas Hardy'. Not the tops perhaps, but better men had done it and survived.

I was called to the Television studios at Lime Grove. I was a little mystified by the T.V. part of the summons, after all I'd applied for a job as a writer in Sound Radio. I found instead that I'd succeeded in becoming an Assistant Floor Manager in Television, whose duties consisted in drawing chalk marks on the floor for the actors and laying out the furniture for rehearsals. It wasn't that I was proud (by this time I more or less agreed with the general tacit assumption of my uselessness) but I hadn't asked for that job, didn't want it, and wasn't any good at it. Still, it was the only one anybody had given me; you could get married on ten pounds a week.

There is something phantasmagoric about this period of my daily life. It all blurs together, saved from nightmare by the evenings with Sally which are clear in my memory. It is as though I became two people, one of whom paid for the happiness of the other. Poor Rosamond, Sally's mother, tirelessly, discreetly kind, managed to find (or invent for all I know) a succession of engagements for the evenings so that we had her flat to ourselves. Never can she have done a kindness that gave more pleasure. Sally cooked supper and we were together, while I tried not to think or talk about the hopeless balls-up I'd made of the day.

It really was a frustrating job. I suppose if I'd hung around for about eight years I might have got to be the man who wears ear-phones and translates the distant director's instructions to the actors: 'He says will you move a bit to the left – Sorry – Hold it – Yes Dick getting you – it's these ear-phones – Sorry old love I mean would you move to the *right*.' It wasn't a thrilling prospect.

The actors were relaxed and friendly, as they always are, so I talked to them and secretly coveted the parts they played. The qualities needed for my particular job were so exactly the ones I didn't possess, there were moments when I wondered wildly if somebody hadn't played a practical joke. These were tasks to be performed mechanically, with unquestioning precision. Most of my colleagues had no time to answer questions anyway – cross, harried men driven for the most part by an intense fear of the sack, and an equally acute sense of their exact position in the hierarchy; the working atmosphere an uneasy marriage of show-biz and the Civil Service.

A programme I looked forward to was 'Puzzle Corner'; every week viewers sent in enormous working models made of match boxes or playing cards or Rinso packets; the one considered most ingenious was shown on the screen. My job was to collect this product of hours of useless labour from the producer's office, and carry it carefully back to the studios. At least it gave me a breath of air.

No doubt of it, London was beating me again. I was determined not to give in without a token struggle and so I pushed every executive's door in the B.B.C. buildings in the hope of finding a loop-hole. The trouble was that I had to fight down so much involuntary self-distaste in order to do this that by the time I was seated in front of the dark-suited loop-hole I couldn't think of a word to recommend myself, distracted by his tiepin or wondering what his home-life was like.

I don't think I was at all unjustly passed over. I really didn't have anything of value to offer my employers. I was just another person, one of millions, stuck in the wrong job.

In the lunch hour I wandered round Shepherds Bush. There used to be a covered market there, and an old pet-shop, the centre piece of which was an ancient bald parrot in a high domed cage. He'd long ago forgotten how to fly and his eyes were bloodshot and full of murder. Staring at him one day he lurched frighteningly at my face and hung upside-down in front of me, making a horrible cracked noise of anger and hatred, his huge beak wide-open, gagging for air; and at the back of his throat his tongue, a blackened stump, moved feebly like an enormous sliced worm, as though it had been torn out at the roots.

·

I had ten pounds a week and Sally had four, a present from her mother who'd given her in trust the savings she'd made from her books. We found a flat, a dank one in Pimlico that smelled of hamsters, and fixed a date to be married. And then, as so often with Sally, the right things began to happen at the right time, like music. We'd neither asked for help nor expected any, but once we'd committed ourselves to a place and a date the help came. An aunt of Sally's who lived in the country decided to buy a house in London and rented it to us cheaply. We converted the top floor into a flat, rented that to a friend, and so we were married and lived rent free in a house of our own. What a joy that was! And marriage itself was like those dreams of flying; you believe so purely and completely that you can, suddenly there you are, circling round the room. It had seemed like a happy end, but it turned out to be only a beginning. I woke each morning to my great good luck, which was itself like a house, endlessly clear and bright, with rooms that continually opened out into larger, brighter ones, unsuspected with Sally singing softly in all of them; that astonishing, musical, heart-easing sound.

Our lives for the next year and a half were too simple to talk about. Sally did odd jobs to help bring in the money. A brief one was looking after some energetic children. That night we came back from some old friends and I was unexpectedly and uncharacteristically sick. Sally felt fine but during the night she had a miscarriage. I took her to the hospital and she was very clouded. I paid her an unexpected visit before work, crept into the ward at seven in the morning. The others were asleep but she was awake, staring at the ceiling. She scarcely recognised me; within seconds she was telling me about the others in the ward, their names, their family histories; not observed, entirely entered into. After a while I realised that many were now awake, smiling on their pillows toward her, not greeting or speaking, just quietly smiling; it was a world she'd made in a couple of days, with her at the centre because of the sheer force of her participation in it. I went out into the courtyard and could have yelled for joy – whereas I suppose I should have been hurt, she'd hardly remembered to say goodbye – but everything I wasn't she so completely was: our one and one didn't make two but two thousand.

Pearse came to stay with us and he asked me how I was. I told him that I was *perfectly happy*. He saw that I meant exactly what I said, and because he understood the person who was saying this amazing thing and had wholly sensed the quality of Sally, his face fell into an expression of the same awe that I was feeling myself. It was as though I'd announced that I'd talked to God.

•

Meanwhile, during the day, I made my chalk marks and my cups of tea. Then I was attached for three whole months to a domestic soap-opera called 'The Grove Family'; I couldn't face this so I resigned, let go this thread that was surely so useless, and sat down and wrote dozens of letters to publishers. We had to eat. These readily showed themselves as uneager for my services as the B.B.C. – both of them are professions over-subscribed by arts graduates. The days in Paris when the world seemed a hinged oyster were a long way gone. Then I struck lucky and was engaged by a firm of book-producers in the production department. I was told that my success was due to the fact that my letter of application had been hand-written and this had much impressed the managing director. If I'd had a typewriter I would have typewritten it. Landing a job, or failing to, is a mysterious business.

I didn't want to read other people's manuscripts when I had so many unwritten of my own, also I preferred reading for pleasure. I wanted to learn a trade, become master of a comfortable corner containing type-faces, Caslon and Baskerville, quires and reams and printing orders. Generously, they sent me off for a couple of months to find out about these things. First, two weeks at a printer's, in Suffolk. I sat next to compositors who'd been on the same stool for forty years, except during the slump in the 'thirties, which it was the anxiety of their lives might happen again. Fine, gentle men incredibly skilful at their work, which they loved. They never read what the tiny pieces of type they were so dexterously putting together were intended to mean. They found it put them off.

Paperbacks were done by machine from beginning to end. As far as I remember the sequence went like this: the sheets are printed on one machine (say sixteen printed pages to the sheet) – then, by conveyor belt, to another machine which folds the sheets, to another which cuts them, then to another which puts a lick of fish-smelling glue along their folded backs. Meanwhile a different set of machines has been printing the covers; the two streams at some point coalesce, covers are attached to the glue and down the chute come the finished books, twenty or thirty a minute, into a sort of dumbwaiter at the bottom, divided into sections. As soon as one section was full a girl at the bottom turned the drum to an empty section. I describe this process because of the girl. She was the only human being in it and that was all she had to do. She was cheaper than the last bit of the machine.

She sat there day-dreaming, absently turning the drum. They only used young girls for the job, they did it till they got married; it paid for frocks and lipstick, but still . . . what a tragic way to spend all your days between eighteen and twenty, your one brief flower. This factory was paternal, benevolent, happy, the August sun was shining on the Suffolk water-meadows outside. But there was this girl looking blankly up at the high bright window in the factory wall – cheaper than a machine. Well, as they say in Russian novels, it's a hard life, why deny it? (It was about this time that I realised my greatest single literary influence had been Constance Garnett. Any chance of a decent style I'd ever had, ruined by my passion for the Russians.) I can't bear to think of that girl, and her millions of brothers and sisters.

The place was full of treasures, dustily packed into drawers; Tenniel's original wood-blocks for *Alice through the Looking Glass* among them. If you penetrated into the recesses of that old family factory you came upon huge storerooms empty but for old typescripts, and first editions of forgotten books, and magazines of the 'nineties, and earlier.

My father had said that Dickens never exaggerated, he only observed, and I think he was right. If you pushed on past the big machines, out of the clanking workshop, past the girl at the bottom of the Penguin chute, you found yourself wandering through these high, silent storerooms, and up the side of one of the most deserted there ran a set of rickety library steps. At the top of these, in a kind of crow's-nest, lived two charming crow-like little men. They were the ones who prepared the typescripts for the press, making sure that foreign words were spelled consistently, and so on. They lived in a blizzard of typewritten paper, pecking into it with their noses, their clothes yellow with age, their eyes yellow, with the angry voracity of birds. They twittered to each other, darting indignantly about in their tiny space among half-finished crusts and scummy tea, passionately pointing out, pages flying everywhere, how this author had italicised a word on page twenty-seven and on page four hundred and six – would you believe it? – had spelled the very same word in roman letters! I wondered if anyone remembered they were still here, in their tree-house. It was impossible to imagine them coming down the stairs, going home. I longed to see them coming on a book of verse by, say, e. e. cummings. Their screeches then would surely become audible; someone might hear and bring them down, clean out the tray at the bottom of their cage.

In the evening I went for walks along the river, through the water-meadows that surrounded that pretty, eighteenth-century red-brick town. It couldn't have changed much since Chateaubriand had stayed with the Vicar during the Emigration and fallen in love with the Vicar's daughter; he'd wanted to marry her. It was a good place to be in love. But mine was as far as ever from finding practical, everyday roots through me. It was like a marvellous balloon, afloat in an atmosphere of its own. I was obsessed with the need to tamp it down, fearful for its safety. This printing – it was interesting enough, but I was only a looker-on – nonsense to pretend there was anything for me here; where was there something then? This was vital – I wanted to care for Sally. But really my attention was elsewhere; I was one of the passengers in the balloon.

I wrote some lines in my hotel bedroom after one of these summer evening walks.

A square-skulled moonfaced monotone fowl
because it is twilight has caught my eye
and slowly insultingly turned its neckless back.
Snubbed by an owl.
One skirt-hem of the sky is torn by day still.
Night continues to mend it, ignoring me.
As I move, nervous against my reason,
there are rustles and splashes I cannot mistake for goodwill.
Blind white moths half my finger-nail size
zig-zag about my feet about no business.
I catch one in my hand, just to make contact
with some part of a world that's mine as well.
It even disdains to flutter,
but waits till I open my hand, then goes on as before.
I feel as though I, hungry,
have entered a room
where there was only just enough to go round.
Because I live in brick and change my clothes
must I allow the world and the sky to ignore me?
Stay, Light! There was something you showed then that I missed!
Well then, come Dark! In your tunnel I'll be more watchful!
What did the river say?

Ordeal by bats is beginning.
How cold this dew is!
So it is really true then
That I neither inhabit this world, nor any other?

.

Men who have managed to lose themselves inside the mystery of their jobs fascinated me. I was sent to the East End of London to learn about colour-printing. Wandering round Cheapside one afternoon, not far from the Tower of London, I caught through the open doorway of a little tumbledown house a glimpse of a furnace. I went in and found two lugubrious young men dressed like pastry-cooks, with round, brimless caps on their heads, pulling out from an oven tiny rolls of metal type. What made the scene extraordinary, even hellish, like the Witch's Transformation scene in a pantomime, was that everything was bright red – their clothes, their faces, the walls, even the ceiling, glowed the colour of blood in the light of the furnace; it was as though the spectrum had gone wrong. They sadly explained that this was due to a powder they used in their work, called, incredibly, Dragon's Blood. They were making the type that goes inside a bus-conductor's ticket machine. That was all they did, the two of them, and they did it for the whole world: Glasgow, Saigon, Tokyo, London. Every so often these towns would obligingly raise their fares, or change their fare-stages or do something which caused the whole business to be done again; they were set up for life, but one of them had doubts: 'I mean, you never really look at your ticket, do you – read it I mean.' They devoted such care to their typesetting and their casting, these two brilliantly encarnadined figures, it seemed a pity. But there were more than two of them – there was the fire and the hissing metal, and all four seemed to work together in a kind of wordless melancholy as though they were lost at the bottom of a dark, red sea.

In the bindery at Wigmore Street they were giving new leather covers to sixteenth- and seventeenth-century books from Lambeth Palace. Putting the title on the new leather spine in gold was a matter of warming the delicate foil over a flame and flicking it with tweezers into position in one movement, the slightest error and it crumbled to nothing; then the letters of the title were pressed on by hand, one by one, the alignment done by eye. The new lettering was so much better than the old, and yet the tools were obviously the ancient ones; I asked why. The binder picked up the three-hundred-years-old spine and examined it critically: 'Oh, Thomas Tofts' (or some such name) 'he must have done this one. Never knew his job.' He may have been coming the old English craftsman over me, but he so obviously was one himself I was very impressed. This world of men working alone, with a high degree of pride and skill, seeking nobody's praise, filled me with admiration.

Then I started work in the office. This was what I wanted, to live according to the rhythm of a great city; rush-hour at each end of the day, and in between, the telephone calls and memoranda, the filing cabinets, the cups of tea, the *Evening Standard*. I must have been mad.

I wanted to write from inside urban life, to have the same problems as everybody else, and I was right to want this. It was the way I set about it that was all wrong. To submerge yourself in the tides of London when you know perfectly well at that stage in your life you're quite incapable of dealing with them, is madness, it's pretending you're someone else. And to try and live like everyone else is a snobbish contradiction in terms. No one around you is living like that, they are all trying to be different.

All over the world there are people stuck in dreary jobs, grateful to have them. But in their very helplessness they band together in their common humanity, they turn themselves into 'us' and the bustling exploiters on the layer above become firmly 'them'. It's possible that way to live with a bit of dignity. But in the fragmented middle-class of London there is no cohesion, no community of feeling. The talk in the bars and restaurants near where I worked was loud and jolly, but always watchful, the competition was still going on under the good-fellowship. It seemed ineffably dreary. By comparison the occasional labourers or lorry-drivers sitting relaxed behind their pints had the quiet self-containedness of another race.

·

A publisher receives a manuscript and publishes it or not as he chooses. A book-producer, on the other hand, is an ideasman. He sells an idea to a publisher and then produces the book for less than he sold it and the publisher puts it out under his imprint hoping to sell it for more than he paid for it. This sounds complicated but is a basically simple device whereby they both stand to make money without much risk of losing any. It all turns round the magical principle of *packaging*. For example: a book-producer gets the idea for a lavishly illustrated (illustrations are always lavish) series of volumes to be called, say 'Animal', 'Vegetable' and 'Mineral': three books. He sells this idea to a publisher who says go ahead. He then hires an editor and tells him how much he can spend on commissioning articles – or rather how little. Someone else collects postcards or reproductions, preferably out of copyright, these are set 'lavishly' amid the cheap articles and the whole is printed in Holland where printing is cheapest. (The fears of unemployment voiced by my old compositors in Suffolk seemed only too well founded.) The whole hotch-potch is given a glossy photographic binding and sold through a publisher who's had all his work done for him, to a public that sees books as objects.

But the packaging process is not finished by any means. The three volumes sell separately and well, because they look like sweets. But why not put all three into a 'slip-case' (a box open on one side into which the three books fit) and sell them as a set, not only here but in America? Further tens of thousands of sets are sold in this way. Nor are we finished yet. Why not get hold of some cheap leather and make a kind of suitcase with a handle, into which you can put the slip-case that contains the three books? Why not indeed, if you can get anybody to buy such an absurd object; but they do, in their thousands, before the first suitcase is even off the assembly lines. Meanwhile everybody gets richer and richer except the people who wrote the words, bought outright at so much a thousand, and the people who made the pictures, most of whom are dead. I suppose it's a harmless enough way to earn a crust but difficult to get enthusiastic about, consisting as it does in selling things not worth having to people who don't really want them.

There was a considerable amount of loot in all this: the managing-director, a downy old bird, was among the first to scent out the existence of this vast, gormless public, and his personal secretary spent most of her day typing out lists of his possessions: silver, furniture, pictures, cellar-lists and so on. She was a depressing creature, no longer young, and so terrified of losing her job that she sped, when called, with such servile haste that she scattered all her carefully collected notes behind her in a shower, and had to return to recover them, getting hopelessly muddled and panic-stricken while her master growled with mounting impatience. Like most women who work in business she was unfairly paid, and lived alone, and in order to save enough to go to the theatre (her one extravagance, her 'hobby' that she clung to proudly) she ate a tired-looking sandwich at her desk instead of going out to lunch. She looked under-nourished and unloved and

I had enough fellow-feeling for her to find her presence almost unbearable. In the course of her struggle with life she had contracted every known tic, twitch, squint and pitch of giggle, as well as several scalp disorders. And there she sat, this piece of human wreckage, typing out a list of somebody else's possessions. You can only go on regarding the school-boy competitiveness of business as a harmless enough way of keeping adults from actually eating each other if you don't have to sit every day next to one of the victims. An election was coming up, and out of genuine curiosity I asked her what way she was going to vote. She was really offended I should even wonder: 'Fancy me voting for those awful common men!' she said.

It would be revealing altogether too squeamish a disposition to say I left that office because I couldn't face the inevitable day when she would get the sack. But her unhappiness leaked all over me, and to sit all day bang next her, typing out that eternal bloody list of objects (she, who had almost been turned into one herself), well, you either have to do something about someone like that (and you can't) or run away. I used sometimes to go into the corridor and do a little dance to remind myself that life wasn't as bad as all that. But for her it was.

At all events, leave I did. The experiment hadn't worked. I'd wanted to give a rhythm to my life, to catch the same buses each day, to walk under the same clock at the same time and know that I would be under it just the same next year. Security, in this sense of rhythm, seemed to me a liberating thing, giving you a quiet margin in which to do your own work. And in fact I was working, meeting other writers, and so on. You have to try these things – how else can you discover you're talking nonsense? And so it was that I looked comfortably up at that clock in the Old Brompton Road one evening and realised that I couldn't stand the sight of it now, never mind next year.

There were other, more important, more delicate reasons to make a change. My marriage was my reason for my life. I had found what I needed, not an extension of myself (by any means) but my counterpart. This is an experience quite unlike any other and therefore difficult to describe. Even the word 'marriage' is a falsification, carrying too many overtones and never used in your own mind in such a situation. You can't talk about feelings, only about their effects. One example will do; a small one but for me a revolution: at this time the Suez war broke out. It struck me as an unjust war; I was on the Reserve but determined not to fight. But more important from my own point of view I found I hadn't the slightest intention of going anywhere near a bullet, and would go to any length whatsoever not to, now. I wanted to live as long as possible. That was the change it had made; for me, enormous. And so through all the disasters of my daily life I blundered about, happy as a lunatic, because whatever happened, I could never be lonely again. And because of the person I knew myself to be I was perfectly aware that the odds against this having happened to me must have been a hundred times greater than the odds against the Treble Chance coming up, and that not in the whole world was it possible to imagine anybody but Sally who could have done this for me.

But here we were living according to the clockwork of London, tired in the evening, dashing off in the morning, looking forward to Sunday. We didn't want always to be together, we lived side by side looking out, not suffocatingly face to face, but this life, now, was absurdly wasteful. Time enough for this when our own tempo had slowed to that of the town or rather when, for distraction, we welcomed the speed of it. But not now, when we had so much to explore in each other, and outside. It was time we tried ourselves out in the world, in different worlds. Our good fortune was also likely to trap us in a narrow layer of Kensington-Chelsea middle-class London, the liberal swaddling indignations of the *New Statesman* and the *Observer* that fell every weekend through the letter-box with an increasingly leaden thump. Our wind was blowing so favourably, so soon, that it seemed a good idea to try spitting into it.

These verbalisations are mine, not Sally's. She could be herself anywhere, couldn't be anything else. Her surroundings took their colour from her, not the other way about. But our thoughts were intermingled on this point. We knew there was something extraordinary between us that shouldn't be shored up by familiarity, the kindness and approval of friends and relatives, not before we'd found out more about it.

And it is true I was getting nervy about my flagrant non-success. My inability to compete amounted almost to a disease. I longed to bring home trophies from the chase; all I had were sad tales about the managing-director's secretary. Sally had healing eyes; just to be looked at by her was to feel blocks of concrete slipping off your chest, in no time at all you were standing upright again. But there was something impatient, almost cruel, not in her, but in her specialness. I had to succeed; not of course necessarily in the world's eyes, but the kinks in my personality had to be straightened out eventually. There is a time limit in such a love, which contains only the barest ingredients of motherliness. For it to remain in its perfect state I had to become my own man.

Meanwhile, what action to take? Teaching seemed a worth-while activity, and England a good place to be out of. The British Council were taking people on permanently about this time, and after various Boards they took me. It was to be either Istanbul or Java. We hoped for Istanbul – Byzantium and so on. We got Java.

Before that a few days in Ireland. In the diagonal rain of a blue Galway, Gort was an echo: Coole Park a clearer one, razed to the ground now. No one anywhere in that driving wet, and then a lonely girl driving a cow. Did she know where Ballylee Castle was (for so it was named on the map); No, she did not, she was sorry, her cheeks shining with rain. Miles on, an old man. Thoor Ballylee? Down there. A grown-over track and there it was, a rotting stump, the windows stolen, dripping blue distemper into the rain. Nettles, trees bending over, encroaching: tiny orchard a wilderness: sea-green slate still in the wall with the poem on it . . . *And may these characters remain/When all is ruin once again.* A tinker had made his fire in the hall and up the winding stair someone somehow had dragged a cart and left it by Yeats' *fin de siècle* wooden fireplace, complex in the simplicity of a vanished fashion. A terrible, brooding place. A monument to imper-manence, triumphant still, in the middle of sucking, humid danger. And then, later, running, running to each other across the lonely, silver, melancholy sands of Mayo. A holy, musical place.

•

We sailed in September 1957. The cabin was filled with flowers from friends. Sally found tooth-mugs and borrowed buckets for all of them, you couldn't move. As we pulled away from the quay-side (she was my responsibility now, I'd taken her up by the roots and we were off, together) the boat gave a lurch and the flowers spilled and smashed; for the first time I felt a touch of fear at what I'd done.

AS SOON AS WE landed and were met it was clear that the man I was to work with had wanted the job I'd been sent out to do. He'd fancied lecturing at the University himself, and me doing the 'administration'.

How that word was to haunt us – haunts the British Council; no long-haired dreamers they. What was it after all? Problems about our own pay and living conditions, occasional arrangements for examinations, scholarships and so on – even the absence of any to do amounted to an obsession.

Anyway he resented me. Not personally; he was an impassioned, round little Welshman with the tiny moist brown eyes of his race, much affected by the heat, jolly to the point of Dylanism on his good days or just after it had rained. But he was what is known as volatile and in his white man's burden mood he retired to brood darkly in the curtained oven of his room, until I became the personification of a London–Oxford plot against himself and then he'd emerge snarling in Welsh, like a corgi.

•

The introduction to Djakarta was not propitious. It is built on a swamp because it is the nearest point to Holland. The natives never had a settlement there, and with reason, the climate is horrible. So is the town the Dutch built, a sprawling suburb without a centre, intersected by useless canals (dug, it seemed, for nostalgic reasons only) which serve as public lavatories and paradisial breeding grounds for rats and cockroaches and mosquitoes. It was hopelessly overcrowded, on every vacant open space little shanty towns had sprung up, even in the middle of public squares, and from these issued hordes of starving, ulcerated beggars who besieged you wherever you went. Administratively it was in chaos, indeed it was under Martial Law, most of the shops were closed, and there was nowhere to live. The houses of Europeans were violated by Army bullies almost every night and the hills around the town were infested with bandits. It was probably one of the nastiest places in the world, but it had its own interest. After the initial sinking of the heart we decided that it was (well, in a way) what we'd been looking for.

We were lent for a few weeks a house that had already been allotted to an official at the Embassy. He'd refused to move in until the air-conditioner had arrived and he allowed us to use it until he considered it habitable. It was situated in one of the more dauntingly European suburbs and he took us there himself; we were met at the door by two smiling and beautiful women who were the servants. He shouted questions at them in English and they grew confused. 'Christ! They're just down from the trees!' he screamed and shoved past them. (It's true that Dickens didn't exaggerate. That's exactly what the man said.) After he had gone away they tentatively regained their smiles, Sally had brought a dictionary and communication was established; all three went happily off to the market together.

The first night in that house was memorable because it

was passed entirely in squashing mosquitoes the size of wasps. My colleague had thoughtfully provided us with a Flit gun, but it proved to have nothing in it.

The University had not yet begun its term so each day I went to the office to administrate. The time would have been better spent preparing lectures, but this was regarded as a spare-time, even frivolous activity. Administration in the abstract was baffling. It seemed to consist largely of putting in urgent pleas for more staff.

First, we set about finding somewhere to live. It is difficult to convey just how important this was; it entered the realm of the metaphysical. Not only did nobody want you there, except a few gentle officials in the Ministry of Education who were powerless, because the Army ran the place. Nature didn't either. A race more imaginative than the Dutch *colons* would have taken the hint long before. The sky was a grey casserole lid with beads of your own steam on it as the dank heat rendered you down, doing curious things to your temper. It was necessary in order actually to *be* in that place to confess at once that you could never be of it. There was no town to float around in and get the feel of. The few bars and restaurants that were still open were empty, or filled with arrogant armed officers. The Europeans were behind closed doors; the natives suspicious or, at best, indifferent. You had to prepare your own patch of favourable soil, plant yourself in it, and hope that some kind of contact would come from that. Otherwise you were reduced to the nervous European pleasures of the diminishing garrison, on whom you were billeted. As nearly as possible you had to start from scratch, which was interesting. It brought us face to face and we learned each other like the first two in a new world.

Gradually, with frequent pauses for despair, we began to make headway. At one point it was necessary to queue for five consecutive days from eight in the morning till two o'clock in the afternoon for a permit that was only a preliminary stage in the process anyway. The town hall was high, with broken windows. Huge fruit-bats the size of buzzards had made their home there and we were all constantly splattered with their dung; the walls were green with it. Every hour or so the door of an inner sanctum would open to reveal laughing be-pistolled officers chatting with each other, cigarettes in long cigarette-holders. The patience of my companions shamed me, and I too learned to sit in a kind of oriental calm, scarcely noticing the passing of the hours. Then I'd spoil it all by getting furiously, occidentally angry.

The bungalow, which was to go with the job, belonged to an unpleasant Chinaman who was getting out in a great hurry; the Government was cracking down on the more obvious parasites. His wife was in Holland and he was off to join her with as much loot as he could salvage. 'Pure Dutch,' he insisted, shoving her photograph at me; his words the ugly, pathetic echo of a faded empire. The illumination in the rooms was entirely pink and green neon, even the table-lamps, heavy wooden dragons with blancmange-coloured tubes spiralling out of each eye. Every window was barred with heavy steel, and the servants' part was cut off by a clanking prison grille.

These bars suggest very well the atmosphere of Djakarta at this time, a shrivelling of the spirit it was hard not to be touched by. A redistribution of wealth was long overdue, and the acquisitive and the quislings had lost their bounce and were ugly and furtive, lived behind bars with a pistol under their pillow, their plans laid for flight before it was too late; meanwhile they were stashing away whatever they could still squeeze. It was astonishing they'd been allowed to get away with it so long, the most remarkable thing about the Indonesians was their forbearance. The problem was, for a European, to make some sense of himself amid so much deserved hostility and contempt.

By dint of filling in forms, making out requisitions, designing bamboo furniture, appealing to precedents, and writing endless memoranda to Bandung (an orgy of administration in fact) we made a start towards this and created something we both needed very much by this time, a clean, well-lighted place from which to make a life. It was not the least of our achievements.

These are details; but in a seasonless tropical country where everything that moves and grows is giant-sized and the same heavy monochrome laurel-green, where the lack of variation beats on your head like a drumstick making your whole sensibility falter, losing certainty, as though you had heat-stroke; in a place where nature moves to encircle you, inexorably, like a snake, you've got to clear your own space in order to live and breathe. Without constant vigilance books, pictures, records are eaten and rot in front of your eyes, posing the question: do these things matter anyway? Everything is struggling to get back to its original primaeval chaos. You let the bats cover you with slime, or you mend the windows. This is above all true in a country which has thrown away a third-rate Europeanism and has not yet found anything to replace it, its own culture buried past revival under three centuries of exploitation.

There is nothing quite so melancholy, or disturbing, as a social machinery that no one knew how to maintain; shops with next to nothing to sell and with dusty, empty windows; large European-style restaurants where the food is inedible because the cooking is imitation European and nobody remembers how to do it; prim gardens reverting to jungle and infested with starving squatters; crumbling pavements fraying off into the residue of broken drains; and the merciless, humid sun that can turn an empty tin-can in the roadway into a heliograph that signals the dissolution of everything. Sad, and obscurely threatening because it puts directly the question: what happens when it all grinds to a halt, what happens in us? It is a far more acute situation than, say, being up the Amazon with the naked head-hunters. There we could have reassured ourselves in terms of what we had left behind. But here there had once been a certain kind of order and now we were witnessing its impermanence, maybe its futility.

Our few possessions took on a special meaning. Brought up to mistrust the density of the tangible world ('travel light'), positively to despise objects and those who attached any importance to them, I saw how much this was a violation of a natural and civilising instinct which had nothing to do with acquisitiveness. I was learning through Sally to respect and trust the series of connections they represented (nothing more, to her they were expendable) and I found myself insisting in the teeth of the jungle, and more, in the rotting jaws of that appalling city, on my right to line our cave. This was not a bourgeois reaction to the tropics, it touched the nerve of survival itself.

That city in its decay represented the very worst in greediness and ugliness that our civilisation can reveal when the wrappings fall away – in every respect it was our, Western European, fault – the necessary outcome of all that had gone before. In the context of the guilt a European must feel in the face of such wretchedness, the act of putting Sally's jug brought from England on top of a bookcase was so absurd it constituted a gesture of faith, accepting the inheritance and trying to assume its responsibilities.

Through the bars of the windows we saw the underside of Europe, what actually happens in the distant place where the money has so magically come from for two or three hundred years, making Europe possible. Sally was the most perfect example of the other side I'd ever seen, the best that could be produced by the culture we belonged to; my unease had tossed her into the middle of my own untidy explorations which for her were simply not necessary; this was the testing ground but my heart misgave me for her, because it was a waste.

Perhaps it needn't have done. We began to build around us and between us the life we had come out to find among people different from ourselves. There was nothing romantic about this, it was the obvious thing to do, and very difficult, but gradually it began to happen. Daunted at first, more than I had been, as I began to experience the full weight of the place and bend under it, she grew in strength and assurance; with her beautiful long bare arms, the fair lock of hair streaked with sweat now, her skin glowing gold with health and pleasure, her brow furrowed over unexpected obstacles, clearing as they cleared.

In the evenings we sat with the windows open, the bars painted white, a spiral smoking in the neck of a bottle to keep the mosquitoes away, while insects vast as aeroplanes crashed and exploded on the white tiled floor. We sat and read, or played a complicated card-game for two that I had a passion for, and drank long iced gins. Outside on the canal bridge boys in imitation baseball jackets quarrelled or plucked hopelessly at un-plugged-in electric guitars (it was the age of skiffle but the ethos had reached Djakarta before the technique), their twangs mixing with the cries and beaten tin-kettles of the street-hawkers running under their balanced poles with a smooth, bent-kneed motion, and the metallic clanging of the frogs and the soft night-time murmurs that came from the squatters' leaf-huts everywhere. In the afternoons Sally sometimes played tennis (execrably) and I more often slept, after a long morning spent bending the ears of my students.

It was a time both peaceful and nervous. It came to me one day (sitting at the filling-station on my way to work) that Sally was stronger than I was; that I depended on her for nourishment now. The days were gone when I could accept her selection of me half-flattered, half-amused. Now, five years after, when our pattern should have been comfortably turning into affection and easy tenderness I was stuck with my blood and lights all blazing in one direction where (if the secret were out) I had no control at all. Possibly the most scarifying thing that can happen is to have your prayers answered. Our wishes, completely fulfilled (which is out of all measure, our desires are always one degree beyond the possible) can have the aspect of an unendurable demand; the hallucinating attraction, mixture of pride and fear, that we feel in front of great natural forces (and this is not to exaggerate, the Romantics were profound in their choice of *locales* – the ocean at night, a storm among mountains): pride in sharing the same world as their sheer size, a morbid desire to hurl ourselves into their centre, and then a sickening sense of our own puniness; a glimpse of what madness might be like.

The balance and the anchoring, the need for the right kind of intensity rooted in life (and not a swooning submission to what sounds like the heart) with no sign-posts save fraying common-sense, it was this that gave the days their special flavour, and sometimes, their fear.

The people we were forced together with at first, Embassy officials and the like, were not the sort you travelled ten thousand miles to find. The women talking constantly of the servant problem, and the men, after so long with their women, half-mistaking the openness of Sally's behaviour for something else, making careful little explorations in that direction, all this bored and irritated me, but not Sally, whom it amused. And she was right as it turned out; the less attractive ones fell away, and others stayed, revealing new aspects of themselves. We even went to the British Club, where the gaze of the wifeless slumped along the bar (their women had been sent home because of the troubles) fastened on her in a way I understood only too well; sometimes I even felt her assaulted by the force of their hot imaginings. I was a life-guard responsible for a treasure, hysterical with alertness, but she floated on their admiration like a mermaid, she could come to no harm.

We played tennis there, even joined the choir (Sally's voice was clear and private, like a nun's). She hadn't any fear of the suburban, or of doing the expected, it was I who was afraid of that, jealous of my differences. But when we met people who would never have gone near that club, and for good reason, it was her they trusted first.

It is strange to stand aside from the person who has become a part of yourself and watch the power they are a vehicle of, which is apart from both of you, expand and develop until it changes the element it finds itself in, like those Japanese paper flowers that feel themselves slowly into every corner of a space, filling with movement and shapes and colours what before was just colourless water. And there was something liquid and yielding about the world she moved through; when anything went wrong, as of course at times it did, she had the forlorn beauty of a stranded mermaid, puzzled, until the waters she knew so well came back to rescue her, and she could call them back herself.

But in all this I knew I had a part. Whatever my self-dissatisfaction I knew I had one gift for sure, an ability to recognise the best when my nose was rubbed into it. Indeed it was sometimes more like a curse, accounting for my restless disappointment with almost everything. But the best I was willing to give my life to, and it needs that kind of service. It is true that beauty is in the eye of the beholder, it needs recognition to be fully itself; appreciation gives it a patina, helps it to bloom. I wasn't a poet for nothing. I had a hand in those marvellous golden lights.

•

There is a layer over the East, for most European eyes, that obstinately remains opaque. There is a passage in one of Rilke's letters that I copied out at this time:

'I have let in so much joy through my eyes; I am so slow in assimilating that I cannot tell what I shall bring home of it. . . . All I know is that one should not be allowed to visit these countries that live their own lives, without a precise purpose; I would almost like to say, without an obvious excuse. . . . It seems to me that especially among the Orientals only the single, hardy traveller of bygone days was admissible: it is grotesque to face this heavy world, which is so entirely enclosed within itself, as an idle protected spectator.'

Though, in Rilke's sense, we had an excuse. I was in fact an employee of the Indonesian Government, a thought which gave me great satisfaction. They paid the British Council a native lecturer's salary, the Council supplemented this and paid me (another source of satisfaction – the terms increased in generosity the more unpleasant the place was supposed to be).

Nationalism is not a very attractive emotion maybe. But these people had been a nation for so short a time, had fought for their independence (1947) so bravely in the face of every kind of betrayal by the Dutch (abetted occasionally by the British) that they were welcome to any help I could give them. They'd been drained dry for three hundred years.

The shareholders of the Dutch East India Company were

paid a fixed dividend; good crop, bad crop, the same amount of money was sent back to Holland. Nothing, or never enough, was put back into the country itself. The only decent buildings on the island were built by Raffles during the five years that remarkable man was there. He laid the roads that are still in use, brought some sort of justice to the laws, founded the Javanese Antiquarian Society and restored Borobodur, that extraordinary, lifeless pyramid of Buddhas the Dutch had allowed to disappear under the jungle. When the Dutch got the East Indies back they took over what he'd done and left it at that; used his roads, kept his legal reforms (because they worked better) and lived in his residence – Sukarno still does – and it remains the only building of merit in the town. Having done nothing for Java for a hundred years, they now proceeded to do exactly the same for another hundred, until they were surprised to find themselves kicked out. It is incredible they didn't concern themselves more with their golden goose. Holland depended almost wholly on the Indies. But there it is, they didn't.

Regarding the Javanese as children (and lacking the aggressive instincts of Europeans they do have an intelligent child-like quality of great strength because they've never lost it), the Dutch didn't educate them or employ them – it was impossible for a native to rise in the public service beyond a humble clerkship – and they still, with truly infantile stubbornness, think of the natives in the same way, as if some day they will repent of their naughtiness and the lovely, almost effortless gold will come rolling in again. I spoke to the Dutch Public Relations Officer on the day the windows in his Trade Legation had been smashed for the umpteenth time and his walls painted with 'Go home Dutch' signs. I suggested his job must be a tricky one. He smiled knowingly: 'Oh – it's all nonsense – they still love us really.' This was so like the English attitude to the Irish, and just as obviously untrue, that I wondered again at the patience of the Indonesians.

About twice a month, during the night, the houses occupied by the remaining Dutch would have painted on them this 'Go home Dutch' slogan. Very rarely was there a mistake, and if there was, if say a British house was painted, the next night, equally mysteriously, the words were distempered over in the correct colour. The Government of course affected to know nothing about all this, but it was so well organised that the whole thing constituted an obvious, and in the circumstances, courteous hint. It was all very decorous. Once a very mild rude word found its way into one of the slogans, and during the day a policeman stood over the offender while he painted it out, leaving of course the rest of it. Occasionally the swollen and inexperienced army got out of hand, but on the whole, watching the behaviour of some of the foreign community, there was no doubt which side was behaving better – and it was the side that now had the power to behave as it liked. But there were still a few pickings left and so these slogans were hints that many of the remaining Dutch chose to ignore, and, after all, many of them had nowhere else to go. In a sense, because they had come too late, these were victims too. Poor people, their houses became more and more fenced in, some of them bought fierce dogs, and in the evening they swapped tales of outrage with each other on the telephone, scarcely daring to venture out; while their servants melted away, or stayed only to steal. The last rags of a colonial régime are not very beautiful.

Never having been allowed the smallest responsibility, it was no wonder that the country was not well run. In fact, what had already been achieved was impressive, and among the first things they had done was to found Universities. It was only after the 1939–45 war that they began to realise what a very small part of the world, of Europe, Holland represented. After the war of independence they decided (for obvious reasons) that English would be a more useful second language than Dutch, and suspicious of too much American influence, entrusted the job of finding the teachers to the politically impotent British Council.

．

To teach English literature in the Far East is obviously in a sense absurd. (And they were spared nothing, there was even a course in Anglo-Saxon.) Apart from anything else it seems impossible for most English writers of the nineteenth century to write a page without mentioning the weather, or to resist heavily overdrawing on the seasons when they want to touch things up a bit. The students obediently wrote down: Spring – Summer, etc., and politely pretended to listen to my despairing explanations as I tried to drown the audible plop of the very natural nothing-whatsoever that was happening in thirty minds. Also, in a new country, people tend to regard a University education as their right, which of course it is. But it wasn't possible not to have doubts about the strictness of the entrance examination in some cases. On the whole, however, the students were intelligent, eager to learn, and very easy to keep amused.

The most difficult thing was to get them to ask questions and so find out whether they'd understood anything or if one was on the wrong track. Their conception of a University derived from some eighteenth-century Dutch pattern in which the teacher played the role of God, they took down his words in silence and then went away and learned them by heart. This disconcerted and depressed me and I battered away at it for months in spite of their dismay for me (I believed the oriental concept of 'face' is best ignored by a foreigner who can never hope fully to enter into it) but it was no use, nobody ever asked a question, they were perfectly happy, had understood everything. At last one day a hand went up, a Chinese boy at the back of the class. Shining with approval and relief I invited him to bring me his sheet of paper, his carefully prepared list of questions. 'Would you answer these please?' He waited humbly, all courteous attention. It was the printed examination paper of the previous year.

In the end I suppose we compromised. Anyway, they no longer gasped with embarrassment when I confessed I didn't know something, and a few even began to offer suggestions themselves. They were delicate, interesting people, trying hard and humbly to enter into a language and culture so distant from their own, and making, it seemed to me, a better job of it than their equivalents in England would have done. The Javanese that is (by which I mean all those from the islands of the Indonesian group, even though they differed very much from each other); there remained unassimilable, unattractive, and working like beavers, the Chinese.

They were middle-class; shop-keepers, money-lenders, tax-farmers, restaurant owners – it was a type the Javanese seemed incapable of producing. I was told, and I believe it, that there wasn't a single café or restaurant in Djakarta that was still run by a Javanese. He was often content to sweep the floor of the place he had once briefly owned, given care of it by the Government after the Dutch had gone. This wasn't incapacity, the students showed in their essays a kind of rare, delicate responsiveness; but it would have been unfair not to give the Chinese better marks when they reproduced, just sufficiently disguised, exactly what one had told them. I confess I didn't like them, they seemed to me a teacher's nightmare – how can you teach a tape-recorder? – and they had the confidence of the materially successful that is the same all over the world. Also they came originally from a part of China that seems to produce an invariably

gross physical type. However, the Javanese wouldn't compete; like the Irish, whom they reminded me of in many
ways, there were certain things they just didn't care enough
about. I was told that every so often the worm turned and
the Chinese were massacred in their thousands. It was possible to understand this.

•

So every morning I taught from eight until about one.
Then, very damp and dry-mouthed (it would be roasting and
thunderous by this time), I'd report to the office where Mel-
vin would greet me with a beer or a file marked 'Urgent'
according to the state of his inner life. Then back to Sally
and a huge delicious lunch. Soedarmi, one of the creatures
just down from the trees, turned out to be the best cook in
Djakarta, with a vast repertoire and an elegant, smiling presence. After that – heat, work and lunch-stunned – siesta; up
about five o'clock, two hours' writing, and then, wage-earn-
ing and self-respect earning both accomplished, the comparative cool of the evening stretches ahead. It was a good
life that was opening up around us, alcohol was cheap and
there were many friends – Pakistani, French, Dutch, Australian, American, Indonesian, English.

And there was Sally. I was beginning to see the world
through her eyes. Her natural responses were so true that I
was able to measure how far mine had become defective and
suspicious, affecting not only the way I experienced but what
– the kind of thing I caused to happen around me. Perhaps
it was true what the man had said, that I had a horizon of
cabbages, but watching Sally there was a chance I could
change that and many other things. The balance between us
shifted. Her perfect involvement in all that happened around
her sometimes caused inside me great lurches of jealousy
and fear. She was not a cosy extension of my own complac-
ence, always to be waiting for me in my kennel, whatever I

did. Whether she stayed there or not depended on whether she wanted to. Loyal to the point of fanaticism, and forever, no one I've ever met has been less capable of pretending to feel something for the sake of convention, or from laziness of habit. I loved this in her particularly. There was no rest, and this for me constituted the reality, for I don't believe there is or should be rest. Being kept on the stretch made becoming tired of being with her an impossibility, she had to be re-won every day, with the joy of probable success that that implied. It was far more likely (and this is where the fear came in) that we would both become tired of me. Secretly, I could scarcely bear to be out of her company. It was becoming possible, after five years, to believe the luck in front of my eyes. I pushed and shoved and pulled and nothing gave; the fabric was solid, the threads held. I trusted my whole weight to it. Nothing that had gone before in my life had prepared me for this, it was a miracle, and I was frightened at the force of it. There is something terrible in loving another person as much as that.

•

Work was going well. I'd never been settled enough before to be able to write each day, and some things I turned out I was willing to stand by. The teaching was all right too, judging by attendances – which you can't, but others do. And always there was this extraordinary girl. Even her clowning grew funnier, not less so. And our head-on collisions, dogged ones, were (if such a thing were possible) like those of Siamese twins, as though our flesh was joined, and not like those of two obstinate people who had chosen to live together, and could still choose otherwise. Sometimes I had to walk away from her in order to prevent the protestations of love, the prostrations, she inspired in me. Perhaps I felt instinctively that it was wrong to feel so much for another human being, or at least to burden them with it. I

don't know why I felt that or why I stopped myself or
whether I was right. Nor do I know now. But this was no
creature of the flat-lands – when I was with her I breathed
air with a flavour of snow.

•

Love is a compendious word as limp as a washing-powder
slogan – Brand X the Mystery Ingredient. It can only be
described in terms of action, which I suppose this book is a
form of. But there were one or two things that surprised me
about it, and if I mention the word I can't duck an attempt
to show what I intend by it.

First of all it wasn't affection multiplied, or infatuation
raised to a higher power; though it contained these things
it was like none of them. Nor did it make me a better person
– or if it did how could I possibly know?

Secondly, its onset (this different thing that has taken hold
of you) is imperceptible. Love may be at first sight (I rather
think it is) but it takes time to realise that it is not all the
other things it is much more likely to be. What I'm describing
is by no means a common human experience, although the
idea that it is, fostered by literature, has caused much confusion. Nor of course is it a mark of merit to have undergone
it.

The surprise is its particularity; this makes it astonishing
that the word should be surrounded by so much vagueness.
It is the least general thing in the world, with a positive
hatred of abstractions. This is why Christianity, pre-emi-
nently the religion of love, has been forced to become the
most concrete of all religions, to the point of absurdity, re-
ducing itself to a series of social precepts. But to brandish a
book of rules in one hand while holding up in the other an
ideal of abstract love that neither preacher nor congregation
can make the slightest sense of, is so inevitable and so in-

tellectually ridiculous that it accounts for the disrepute of the word itself, and its descent into near-meaninglessness.

An example of this particularity: there are objects in this room that Sally has touched. These, to my eyes, are more themselves than others she hasn't. I can throw one of these enhanced objects out of the window without pain (or any pain is my own, nothing to do with the case) but it will not cease to be different, to have a degree more meaning; and there is nothing sentimental about this.

This particularity, of course, extends to the person themselves. Everything seen and felt in the context of the emotion I'm talking about appears to take on its full reality for the first time. You're still as much of a fool, but you're a real fool.

Another aspect of it, the most essential and surprising of all, is that you know at the time that it is not in you to feel this way twice – so far removed is any sense of generality. There can be only one object, not only for this intensity, but for this feeling. From there it may be possible to move outwards, but the centre can never be in more places than one.

Does this love for one person make it easier for you to love others? I don't think so – you still have yourself to contend with.

Is it possible that your inability to love anyone else in the same way (assuming this to be true) is a piece of self-indulgence, clutching what you feel to yourself like a medal, or an acre of land?

Possible. . . . So?

The courage required to face facts, to come to terms with reality (measured I don't know by what standard, the Concentration Camps perhaps, which have blurred all measurement) has an air of sinewy maleness. But it's as easy to exaggerate in the direction of smallness as it is in the other.

This 'acre of land' for instance, might just as well be room enough for a lifetime's cultivation and exploration, one man's great estate.

.

We took trips into the hills and to Jogjakarta, which had been, in a sense, the native capital. It was beautiful and cool and unlike Djakarta had a life of its own. I gave some lectures at the University there and they asked me to join them, full time, no 'administration'; even that was sorting itself out. But although in Jogjakarta there were dancers and painters and musicians, remnants of the old Javanese life and the first stirrings of a new one, we didn't take a decision straight away. Djakarta was too easy to desert. Sally taught now as well and her pupils multiplied alarmingly, like rabbits. I plugged away at the nineteenth century, the factory conditions, the struggle for reform, because this really interested the students, nearly all of whom had some experience of sudden, chaotic industrialisation. Neither of us thought we were doing much, but we were in the middle of it all, the expanding world of the mid-twentieth century, and learning. The ancient ways were less important than what was happening in front of our eyes.

.

We went for a few days to Bali, which means 'holy'. Another holy island like the other on the far side of the world. 'You'll never get there,' we were told, or, if we should arrive safely, 'You'll never get back'; the foreign communities in Djakarta lived in a state of siege. However, the Indonesians we knew seemed to think it would be all right and told us of a Balinese rajah, called a Tjokoerde, who put up visitors. So we wrote him we were coming, not very hopeful he'd ever get the letter; but sure enough he was there, waiting to meet us.

Unlike cultured Javanese, who tended towards skin and bone, as though they dined on their own abstractions, he was a fleshy jolly little man with an explosive giggle. He presented a bizarre appearance; from the waist down he was wearing a batik sarong, above the waist an open-necked European shirt in pastel stripes, and on his head perched at a slightly drunken angle a brightly coloured turban with a hole in the middle like a deck-quoit.

He looked after us very well. His palace was a series of carved thatched huts round two courtyards, and in the second of these, all night it seemed, among heavy-scented trees whose blossoms glowed blue in the dark, the gamelan orchestra played. One notices the usual things about Bali, the people are beautiful; look closer and they are poor and diseased as well. But it is this constant music that shuts up the observing European in you, and was for me at any rate the new experience. They go on all night, these complex syncopated rhythms on drums, gongs and different sizes of a kind of brass xylophone, rising to a crescendo and then unpredictably, in what sounds like mid-phrase, stopping altogether; until somebody else begins to doodle ruminatively on his instrument. They sit slumped on a covered platform in the courtyard lit by tapers; some of them doze. They're rice farmers come in from their fields; this is their way of passing the evening, every evening. Their technique is such, their ear is so practised, that one of them can wake up and come in perfectly on an improvisation, amuse himself with it and sign himself out; it's a jam session, formal, relaxed and very sophisticated. They take time off to eat a scrap of rice on a palm leaf sitting at their instrument – like the Javanese they don't have mealtimes, just eat when they feel like it – or yawn and stretch or talk to a neighbour, while the man on the other side is working out a private musical

conundrum. Someone else might give him a hand, do the
harmonics; if it sounds interesting they'll all gradually join
in and they're off again.

When the musicians have to play at a feast their neighbours
look after their fields for them; and they perhaps look after
the sculptors' fields when the statues need refurbishing, as
they regularly do, scattered everywhere, traditional Hindu
gods and goddesses carved out of soft crumbling volcanic
tufa stone. Everyone was paid in work, not money; the man
who forged the iron for the instruments, the man who provided his tree for the new gong-stand. The iron itself had to
be bought from Java and the whole village contributed to
that.

Out of the scented dark round the musicians, into the light
of the tapers, ran thin scraps of girl-children, bits of brown
sacking tied round them, tucked up under their armpits. And
they'd practise their steps, bending their tiny hands backwards in crescents, moving their heads from side to side
parallel with their shoulders. Sometimes an older girl ran
out of the shadows and stood behind one of them holding
her arms, doing the dance herself, using the child as a puppet
so that the dance entered into the child wordlessly, the movement married directly to the music. There was no rebuke for
a mistake, concentration was gentle and smiling and abso-
lute. Even when the movements of the dance brought them
within inches of our strange faces they paid no attention,
their darting eyes obeying only the music, the dance. Then
they'd disappear as unpredictably as they'd come – the music
would lapse or go on – nothing was predictable.

It got into you that music, much of the day and most of
the night, changing, broken rhythms and half-rhythms marking every point between melancholy and communal aban-
don. You felt the crisp, sure lines of your Western sensibility
begin to yield and blur. The music and the dance perfor-

mances never had a clearly defined beginning or end and at first this unexpectedness was like an affront, allowing you no time to collect yourself properly to watch and listen. But in an almost seasonless country with the same hours of daylight and darkness all the year round, time doesn't press and threaten, is seen more clearly as a flux, a river, and the performers and the villagers seemed quite clearly to be waiting half-consciously for the perfect moment to embark. And to sit collected on your chair was already to be in the wrong frame of mind to understand something which is communal expression, arising directly out of the needs of audience and performer alike, not presented to them for their understanding or distraction. It wasn't Time but the evil spirits that had to be put in their place, for they can corrupt pleasure, so through the crowd their caricatures dance and gibber, dressed in masks that are half-frightening, half-comic, making the children scream delightedly, uncertainly, and their parents laugh, just as we used to laugh at cartoons of Adolf during the war.

The Tjokoerde took us to a neighbouring village for a great festival. We arrived in the early morning and all day girls in yellow sarongs filed past us up to the temple carrying on their heads their pink and white offerings of painted rice-flour cooked into intricate shapes. We sat in a house and waited, out of the sun. In front of us was a girl with a little sweet-stall and beautiful careless breasts. The hours passed; no one knew when anything would happen or where, or whether in fact anything would, and didn't seem to mind very much; they were all Balinese, the owners of the house, relations of the Tjokoerde. We just sat in the bare, shadowy room in the little brick house on kitchen chairs arranged in a square and waited. Darkness fell, the girl outside lit a taper at her tiny stall and covered her shoulders; the stalls all round the square lit their tapers, the crowd who'd been arriving all day from the outlying villages sat in the shadows whispering and laughing. At last there was movement in the back of the house – yes, it would happen, the dancers had arrived, and the flute orchestra. The news spread outside and all the dogs in the village began to bark, the terrible, staring Balinese dogs, covered with sores, and with tiny shrunken heads like overgrown rats.

We watched the dancers being made up and tied into their ceremonial costumes by older women while the flute orchestra blew a mysterious keening Irish note in the darkness of the yard at the back of the house.

And then to a mud-floored hall, crowded as only an oriental hall can be – people were courteously climbing over each other's faces. Space was somehow found for us (our Tjokoerde was Headman here as well and a very comic-looking one. For this day's outing away from home he'd provided himself with a straw handbag tucked under his arm and with his sarong and his crazy turban he looked as though he was off for some Christmas shopping at Selfridge's.) The dressed-up girls were among the crowd, and the flute players, and the local gamelan orchestra. Somebody struck a chord and nothing happened. The girls were on the floor now, but talking to the crowd, the music started, still no dancing, and then, as though a mysterious point of concentration had been reached, absently waited for by everybody like a visiting angel, the performance began.

I remember nothing of the dance itself, which was a Butterfly one, rare apparently, except the casual unexpected beginning which always surprised me, the absence of Curtain Up. And that the girls' wings were painted like butterflies only on the upper side, the one least often seen because they danced with their arms raised, and fluttered the dark, unpainted sacking at us, and that nobody had swept the mud floor. Their naked feet curled among dropped rice and spit, chewed bones and dogs' urine and worse. One of these dogs, objects of dread, tolerated only because they scared evil spirits away, brushed under Sally's long legs, its back blue and green with running sores. She didn't see it. She was staring, with a kind of illumination in her face, at the dancers.

'Now I feel like a *real* traveller,' she said in a strange voice, staring in front of her. Surprised – Sally was never banal – I was caught by something in the look of her. Then I saw what she meant, and then it happened to me.

It takes time to reach such moments: the previous years, the last strange months, and the long hours spent just now in that bare, patient house, they'd done their work. Things had come together. We were there in that room, with the others, not looking on; the angel had visited us too. The spools of the threads that joined us to our separate pasts, pulled upon, had slowly proved themselves of infinite length. We were free; what there was between us was paid for now, and ours. In that way we'd become travellers; now there was only us.

•

Every shade of violent green, white tumbling cascades, blossoms everywhere, red, luminous blue-white, fragile yellow; twirled in fingers, stuck in hair, lying casually, offerings in front of tiny shrines, or on the table, decorating the food. The omnipresent gods invited to share the meal, a small portion set aside for them on a banana leaf in front of the statue each time of eating; evil spirits to be warded off. Ducks, erect as commas, driven by boys with long sticks they waved over the procession like a mesmerist, the squad obeying the movement as one duck; black, half-wild pigs rooting everywhere like minature boars; dogs . . . dogs.

Sally stumbled and fell as we balanced our way along the narrow dykes between paddy-fields. She scratched the inside of her arm on a kind of cactus and I was impatient. There were times when she made exploration impossible, banging into things, falling over, as though her body was being pulled out of sync, pulled down; she became heavy. The scratches weren't deep but they glowed red, and stayed even after we'd left Bali, as though there'd been some poison in the spines, and I was sorry I'd been angry. But there were these times, that always strained my patience because they frightened me, when it was nearly impossible to walk along an empty pavement, she tripped over invisible objects, as though the contradictions and darknesses that slither inside us had decided to attack her from another angle, and were pulling at her from outside. What bewildered me was that she struggled, whereas I would have had her sit and wait for this thing to pass, whatever it was.

We went to the sea, to a deserted hotel, we were probably the only visitors on the island. We arrived at evening and caught our breath. White coral sand, pink sea, naked girls playing in it under the sunset. They see us and vanish, laughing, calling out to each other, take flight like small dark birds. Almost in front of us the blunt symmetry of the Gunung Agung, the sacred volcano, skewers the last of the burning clouds on the other side of the bay.

In the morning our room, which opened on to the sand itself, was filled with a soft pink glow. We stepped out to watch the dawn over the sea. For some reason I wrote down the sequence of this one '5.30. Sky a dull pink shading to blue; long streaks of cloud in soft grey wash – a child's impatient attempt at monsters with the water the brushes have been cleaned in. 5.50. A red fuse burns along the bottom of the clouds, then along the top until they are dark grey, edged all round with red, over a silver sea. Behind, to the west, a black cloud goes yellow. Now there's a burning thumbnail in the middle of the sea. In two minutes a perfect ball balances for a second on the horizon and then floats up.

The sea is yellow, the sky is blue, the clouds a brighter yellow. Day. 6 o'clock.'

I watched Sally. She sat in her nightdress on the warm soft sand, violet and gold, staring out over the sea, her knees drawn up to her chin. Things had changed between us. I was gathering my strength from her now, she was wordlessly explaining the world to me, gathering me into it, teaching me how to love it. But this strength she gave me would be hers to use again when it was her turn to lag. I watched her, the dawn and the sea.

Back in Djakarta the Cambridge examinations began. These are public examinations in English set up by Cambridge University and have to be invigilated according to Cambridge rules. Sitting on a dais looking down on the long lines of scribbling, frowning, white-clad figures, I doodled. To go to Jogjakarta, or not? There were friends here . . . things going well . . . Sally's pupils . . . I sketched some lines about the holiday and about us. A whispering colleague arrived to take over. It was all very reminiscent of exams in England, only this time it was me, lordily dreaming up on the dais. 'Half an hour more.' Voice booming pleasingly into the silence. Gasps, redoubled scratchings.

Outside I glanced at the lines I'd written. They didn't seem too bad. I collected Sally from her shopping and showed them to her. They were the first I'd written directly about her for three years or so.

> *Curled in your night-dress on the beach,*
> *Corn-yellow ghost, pale with sleep,*
> *Head to the starry North, bare toes to the burning East,*
> *Tracking the Sun's climb into our seaside perch,*
> *I watch you at the fringe of this other island*
> *Our public love makes private for two;*

Your face in floating shadow like a moon,
Stretching your arms around the bay to yawn,
Ebony trees in your finger turning to green.
I stand alone, in the dark, with the birds in the bush.
Like the pewter lagoon I am flustered by day,
Which turns, turns, like a pin to prick out my eye.
Now Sun, the angry bo'sun, straddles the sea.
'Is that you?' your murmur,
Grateful and blind my whisper,
'You and me.'

She didn't quite take them in, she had a headache. I told
her not to go to her pupils that afternoon, but she said she
didn't feel that bad. In the evening she was no better and
the doctor diagnosed 'flu. After a couple of days there
seemed no improvement but the doctor still said 'flu. Next
day I realised Sally was ill although she didn't think so herself
and the doctor examined her again and took me outside and
told me she had polio.

In the morning I took her in to hospital and chased round
for other doctors, and the Embassy laid on an aeroplane
standing by in Singapore. At the hospital the doctors arrived
and conferred and told me for the moment best not to move
her and that there was no need to worry, these things could
often pass off with no damage at all. I stayed with her while
she slept and at four o'clock in the morning, midsummer's
day, Sally died.

THE STORY DOESN'T end there, of course, but this one has to, for it's the story of a recognition and a rescue, in terms of our two lives.

When I sat for a while in the dark among the knobbled roots of some great Javanese tree that grew alone in the quadrangle of the hospital, just outside the narrow strip of light that fell on the verandah from Sally's room, I felt the roots under my hands and watched the thin spray of light from the room and looked up through leaves into the thick, curving night. Then I went back into the room and the doctor almost shouted 'Your wife is dead you know!' as though to someone deaf, his heavy Dutch face lowering into mine, and I had to keep from smiling politely because he obviously expected something from me and it couldn't have been that. I did know, and the knowledge was my tunnel, waiting outside for me to walk down it. But just for this moment I'd never been closer to life and to Sally. What I'd felt under my hands when I sat in the roots of the tree, or what I'd seen when I stared up, I couldn't be sure, but it wasn't this hospital sense of death. It had been a rhythm and spaciousness, a power that leaped through gulfs of darkness beaming a series of connections, and my mind had snapped over those flashes like a lid. What I had seen I had seen; one day, if I kept silence and watched, it might belong to me, move in my blood like lymph so that what had happened had happened to both of us, making sense of both our lives and sense of life, turning what seemed an end into a beginning, even (and this I'd glimpsed humbly, understanding nothing) suggesting that every end, for the living as for the dead, can be the form of an initiation. There was a chance in that kind of journey down the tunnel; in any other kind there was no chance at all.

·

I haven't any conclusions to offer. I mistrust other people's too much to try any of my own. A man believes different things at different times, or perhaps different versions of the same thing. Most of us suspend the question and try to live in the present which is only today's version of the past.

The house I'm outside as I write this was built by men who are dead. All my life I've been feeding on the ideas of dead men. So it is impossible to imagine my present without the sustaining, confusing past, without Sally. To turn her into a memory would be impossible, there are some persons, some events, it isn't possible to shrink in this way; they're outside our range.

I have felt her presence so powerfully at times that I've found it easy to believe a great many things. The sky would not have held all the things I could believe. It comes, it goes, it will come again, and it leaves a residue. Once you've experienced the infinite significance of another person's life you feel something of the same for all lives, and for your own. There remains in the world this infinite significance and to every event we owe a responsibility. Also we must forgive ourselves. You can construct a universe out of that, a heaven and a hell.

Sally is buried in England, in Westwell where we often

went together. Perhaps these things aren't important, but it helped me at the time. A proper attitude to death, if we can find it, is a source of life. I'd like to be buried next to her. Again, I know it doesn't matter, but it pleases me to think it might happen. I noticed last Christmas (it isn't far from here) that there's no room on the stone for another name. I don't care whether my name appears on it or not but it might cause confusion when the time comes, if there's anybody about who cares tuppence either way; which is why I began all this by saying I'd had to make arrangements about my gravestone, which is hers. But I found I couldn't do it, couldn't think that way. This is my memorial to what happened between us, made, as I say, out of bits and pieces lying around me, bits of myself, all I had to bring her. Or rather, it's part of it. The rest of my life, any sense I can make of it, is a memorial to that.